AI Agriculture in China
Haiqing English Chinese Bilingual Series

By Haiqing Hua

haiqinghua@yahoo.com

Haiqing Hua | LinkedIn

Table of Contents

32. Fields of Automation

The Pioneer: Li Wei and the Future of Agricultural Expert Systems

In a bustling city nestled among China's agricultural heartlands, Li Wei, a quiet but determined computer scientist, found himself drawn to the fields just as much as to his algorithms. Growing up in a rural village, he understood the challenges farmers faced: the unpredictable weather, the delicate balance of soil nutrients, and the ever-evolving pests that threatened crops.

Driven by a deep-rooted passion to bridge technology and agriculture, Li Wei embarked on a journey that would redefine farming in China. Armed with a formidable intellect and a vision for sustainable agriculture, he founded a small startup dedicated to developing AI-driven systems tailored for farmers.

Initially met with skepticism from traditionalists who doubted the role of technology in farming, Li Wei persisted. He immersed himself in understanding the intricate details of agricultural practices, blending his technical expertise with practical insights from local farmers.

His breakthrough came with the creation of an innovative agricultural expert system. Combining machine learning algorithms with real-time data from local farms, the system offered personalized recommendations to farmers, from optimal planting times to precise pesticide application, all aimed at maximizing yield while minimizing environmental impact.

As word of his system spread, Li Wei's startup flourished. Farmers who once relied solely on ancestral wisdom now turned to his AI-driven solutions for guidance. Fields that once struggled with inefficiencies and unpredictability now bloomed with efficiency and resilience.

Yet, Li Wei's journey wasn't without challenges. Navigating the complexities of rural China's infrastructure, from internet connectivity to farmer education, tested his resolve. Undeterred, he partnered with local governments and agricultural cooperatives to expand access to his technology, ensuring that even the most remote farmers could benefit.

Over time, Li Wei's work not only transformed agriculture but also fostered a new generation of tech-savvy farmers. Inspired by his success, young minds from rural communities began pursuing careers in agritech, eager to contribute to China's agricultural revolution.

Today, as Li Wei reflects on his journey from rural roots to technological pioneer, he remains committed to pushing the boundaries of what's possible. His dream of creating a sustainable future for Chinese agriculture continues to drive him forward, reminding all that innovation, when rooted in empathy and understanding, can truly change the world, one harvest at a time.

先锋者李伟与农业专家系统的未来

在中国农业核心区域的繁华城市中，李伟，一位安静而坚定的计算机科学家，发现自己同样被田野吸引，就像他被算法所吸引一样。他在一个农村村庄长大，深知农民面临的挑战：不可预测的天气、土壤营养的微妙平衡，以及威胁农作物的不断变化的病虫害。

出于对将技术与农业结合的深厚热情，李伟踏上了一段重新定义中国农业的旅程。凭借强大的智力和对可持续农业的愿景，他创立了一家专注于开发为农民量身定制的人工智能系统的小型初创企业。

最初，传统主义者对技术在农业中的作用持怀疑态度，对李伟的创新持怀疑态度。他沉浸于理解农业实践的复杂细节中，将技术专业知识与来自当地农民的实际见解相结合。

他的突破是通过创建创新的农业专家系统实现的。该系统结合了机器学习算法和来自当地农场的实时数据，为农民提供个性化建议，从最佳种植时间到精确的农药应用，旨在最大化产量同时最大限度地减少环境影响。

随着他系统的声誉传播开来，李伟的初创企业蓬勃发展。曾经仅依赖祖传智慧的农民现在转向他的 AI 驱动解决方案寻求指导。曾经因效率低下和不可预测性而苦苦挣扎的田地现在因其系统的智能化而充满了效率和抗灾能力。

然而，李伟的道路并非一帆风顺。他在解决中国农村基础设施的复杂性方面，从互联网连接到农民教育，都对他的决心进行了测试。尽管如此，他与地方政府和农业合作社合作，扩大了农民接触他技术的渠道，确保甚至最偏远的农民也能受益。

随着时间的推移，李伟的工作不仅转变了农业，还培养了一代新的科技型农民。受他成功的启发，来自农村社区的年轻人开始追求农业技术领域的职业，渴望为中国的农业革命贡献力量。

今天，当李伟回顾他从乡村到技术先锋的旅程时，他依然致力于推动技术创新的边界。他对创造中国农业可持续发展的梦想仍然推动着他前行，提醒所有人，创新，当以情感和理解为根基时，真正可以改变世界，一次丰收一次。

**In fields of gold, where sunlight streams,
A silent helper weaves its dreams.
No hands of toil, no farmer's sweat,
But lines of code, a digital net.**

**The Expert System, wise and vast,
Holds knowledge from the ages past.
Of pests and plagues, of soil and seed,
It whispers secrets, helps us succeed.**

**With sensors keen, it scans the land,
Moisture levels, at its command.
Nutrient needs, it calculates,
A tailored plan, for fertile crates.**

Diseases lurk, a silent threat,
But patterns matched, the system's met.
A spray prescribed, a timely dose,
To save the harvest, from nature's woes.

From sunlit fields to screens aglow,
The bridge is built, for knowledge to flow.
The farmer's friend, unseen, unheard,
A silent hero, each whispered word.

So let us raise a digital toast,
To lines of code, that help the most.
For in this dance, of man and machine,
A greener future, we can glean.

金色麦田，阳光流淌，
静默助手，编织梦想。
非农夫汗水，非劳作双手，
代码编织，数字罗网。

专家系统，智慧广博，
储存古今，知识浩渺。
虫害病害，土壤种子，
悄声密语，助我们成功。

传感器敏锐，扫描土地，
湿度水平，尽在掌握。
营养需求，精准计算，
量身定制，丰收硕果。

疾病潜伏，无声威胁，
系统匹配，化解危机。
精准喷施，及时剂量，
拯救收成，摆脱天灾。

从阳光麦田到屏幕亮光，

知识桥梁，畅通无阻。
农民挚友，不见不闻，
每个字语，默默守护。

数字祝酒，高举杯盏，
赞颂代码，助我们力量。
在人和机器的协作舞动，
共迎未来，一片绿漾。

Fields of Transformation

In the heart of rural China, where vast fields stretched under the expansive sky, a transformation quietly unfolded over the past three decades. Since the beginning of economic reforms, the countryside had witnessed a revolution as profound as the changes in the city skylines.

Liu Yong stood at the edge of his family's wheat field, watching the sun rise over the distant mountains. His weathered hands, once calloused from years of manual labor, now grasped the handle of a modern tractor, a symbol of the technological leap that had reshaped farming in their village. The fields, once tilled by generations before him with simple tools, now yielded abundant harvests thanks to irrigation systems and improved seed varieties.

"Grandfather used to tell me stories of how they plowed the land with oxen," Liu Yong mused to himself, adjusting his cap against the morning breeze. "Now, we have machines that do the work in a fraction of the time."

Indeed, the economic reforms had not just boosted urban industries but had also revitalized rural life. Villages once isolated were now connected by paved roads, allowing for easier transportation of goods and services. Schools and clinics had sprung up, ensuring that children received education and families had access to healthcare previously unimaginable.

As Liu Yong drove the tractor along the rows of ripening wheat, he reflected on the changes he had witnessed. The annual growth rates of over 9% had not just been numbers in reports but had translated into tangible improvements in his community. Income from farming had risen steadily, enabling families to afford modern amenities and invest in their children's futures.

"We used to worry about having enough to eat," Liu Yong recalled, a faint smile touching his weathered face. "Now, we worry about how to expand our operations and improve yields even further."

The advancements in agriculture had not only fed China's vast population but had also positioned the country as a global agricultural powerhouse. From exporting rice and vegetables to technological innovations in farming equipment, China had become a beacon of agricultural success.

But amidst the progress, Liu Yong knew challenges remained. Climate change threatened to disrupt seasons, and market fluctuations posed risks to their livelihoods. Yet, the spirit of resilience and adaptation that had guided his ancestors through generations of hardships now fueled their determination to overcome new obstacles.

As the sun climbed higher in the sky, Liu Yong's thoughts turned to his children, who were studying in the city with dreams of careers beyond the fields. He hoped they would carry forward the legacy of hard work and innovation that had transformed their family's fortunes.

Standing in the midst of his flourishing fields, Liu Yong felt a sense of pride—not just in what they had achieved but in how far they had come. The reforms had not only nourished their bodies but had also nurtured their spirits, instilling hope and optimism for a future where rural and urban China continued to thrive together.

With a deep breath, Liu Yong turned the tractor toward the next task, knowing that with each plow and each seed sown, they were not just farming the land but cultivating a brighter tomorrow for generations to come.

This story explores the profound changes in Chinese agriculture and rural life since the economic reforms began, highlighting both the challenges and the remarkable achievements that have reshaped the countryside.

变革的田野

在中国广袤的田野上，随着经济改革的开始，过去三十年间，一场悄然的变革正在农村深处悄然发生，这场变革与城市天际线的变化一样深远。

刘勇站在家族的小麦田边，眺望着远处群山上升起的朝阳。他那双经历了多年体力劳动而变得粗糙的双手，此刻握着一辆现代化拖拉机的把手，这是农业技术飞跃的象征，它重塑了他们村庄的农耕方式。曾经祖辈们用简单工具耕种的田地，如今由于灌溉系统和改良的种子品种，产量丰收。

"爷爷曾告诉我他们如何用牛耕种地。"刘勇自言自语，调整着头上的帽子抵挡清晨的微风。"现在，我们有了可以在极短时间内完成工作的机器。"

的确，经济改革不仅推动了城市工业的发展，也为农村生活带来了前所未有的改善。曾经孤立的村庄现在通过铺设的道路相连，便利了物资和服务的运输。学校和诊所如雨后春笋般涌现，确保孩子们接受了以前难以想象的教育和家庭拥有了健康保障。

当刘勇驾驶拖拉机沿着一排排正在成熟的小麦行驶时，他在思考着他所见证的变化。超过9%的年度增长率不仅仅是报告中的数字，它们也转化为了社区中实实在在的改善。农业收入稳步增长，使得家庭能够拥有现代化的生活设施，并投资于孩子们的未来。

"过去我们担心是否能够吃饱，"刘勇回忆道，他苍老的面庞上露出了淡淡的微笑。"现在，我们担心的是如何扩展我们的经营和进一步提高产量。"

农业的进步不仅仅是为了满足中国庞大的人口需求，还将中国定位为全球农业强国。从出口大米和蔬菜到农业设备技术创新，中国已经成为农业成功的典范。

然而，在这一进步的背后，刘勇知道仍然存在挑战。气候变化威胁着季节性的稳定，市场波动对他们的生计构成风险。然而，他们祖辈通过代代传承的坚韧和适应精神，现在正激励他们克服新的障碍。

当太阳在天空中升高时，刘勇的思绪转向了在城市学习的子女们，他们梦想着超越田野的职业生涯。他希望他们能继承努力工作和创新精神的传统，这种精神不仅改善了他们家庭的命运，也为农村和城市中国持续繁荣的未来注入了希望和乐观。

站在丰收的田野中央，刘勇感到一种骄傲——不仅仅是对他们所取得的成就的骄傲，也是对他们所走过的漫长道路的骄傲。改革不仅仅滋养了他们的身体，也培养了他们的精神，灌输了对未来的希望和乐观情绪，在农村和城市中国继续共同繁荣的明天。

刘勇深吸了一口气，将拖拉机转向下一个任务，他深知每一次耕作和每一粒播种，都不仅仅是在耕种土地，更是为子孙后代开辟一个更加美好的明天。

这个故事探讨了中国农业和农村生活自经济改革以来的深刻变化，突出了农村面临的挑战和取得的显著成就，重塑了乡村的面貌

In fields of green, where life takes root,
A silent change, a hidden fruit.
Not verdant growth, nor blooming pride,
But hearts and minds, where dreams confide.

These fertile grounds, once fallow lay,
Now tilled by thoughts, to pave the way.
From doubt and fear, a seedling sprouts,
Nurtured by hope, dispelling droughts.

The sun of knowledge, warm and bright,
Shines on these fields, banishing night.
With lessons learned, and wisdom sown,
Old patterns fade, new truths are known.

A gentle rain of empathy falls,
Washing away the rigid walls.

Forgiveness blooms, where anger burned,
Compassion thrives, where lessons learned.

The fields of change, a wondrous sight,
Where caterpillars morph in flight.
From limitations, wings unfold,
Embracing strength, a story told.

So let us tend these fields with care,
Where transformation fills the air.
For in this growth, a future lies,
Where hearts take flight, and spirits rise.

在绿意盎然的田野，生命扎根，
悄无声息的变化，隐藏的果实。
并非翠绿的生长，也非盛开的骄傲，
而是心与智的沃土，梦想在此诉说。

这片曾经贫瘠的土地，如今松软肥沃，
思想耕耘，开辟道路。
从怀疑和恐惧中，幼苗萌生，
希望的滋养，驱散干旱。

知识的太阳，温暖而明亮，
照耀着这些田野，驱散黑暗。
汲取教训，播种智慧，
旧有的模式消退，新的真理被认知。

同理心的细雨落下，
冲刷掉僵化的墙壁。
宽恕盛开，愤怒曾经燃烧的地方，
汲取教训，慈悲茁壮成长。

变化的田野，令人惊叹的景象，
毛虫蜕变，展翅飞翔。
从局限中，翅膀展开，

拥抱力量，诉说故事。

让我们精心照料这些田野，
让蜕变充盈空气。
因为在这片成长中，蕴藏着未来，
心灵翱翔，精神升起。

Harvest of Dedication

In the heartland of rural China, amidst rolling fields that stretched as far as the eye could see, Li Wei stood as a testament to dedication and progress in agriculture. Born and raised in a small village where farming was not just a livelihood but a way of life, Li Wei had always felt a deep connection to the land.

From a young age, he witnessed the toil and sweat of his parents and neighbors as they worked the fields using traditional methods passed down through generations. Yet, Li Wei harbored a dream - a dream of transforming their labor into something more efficient, more productive.

Driven by curiosity and a thirst for knowledge, Li Wei pursued studies in agricultural science against all odds. His journey was not easy. It meant leaving behind the familiarity of his village, enduring hardships in pursuit of education, and challenging conventional wisdom in agriculture.

Years later, armed with a degree and a vision, Li Wei returned to his village not as just another farmer, but as a harbinger of change. He immersed himself in research, collaborating with scientists and experts to harness the power of technology for rural development.

His breakthrough came with the introduction of precision farming techniques. Armed with drones and satellite imaging, Li Wei revolutionized how crops were managed. No longer were farmers reliant solely on weather patterns and traditional wisdom; now, they could make data-driven decisions that optimized yield and minimized environmental impact.

But Li Wei's contributions went beyond technology. He became a champion for sustainable farming practices, advocating for organic methods that preserved soil health and biodiversity. His efforts didn't just increase productivity; they revitalized community spirit and instilled a sense of pride among farmers who saw their hard work translate into tangible results.

As seasons passed, Li Wei's name became synonymous with innovation and progress in Chinese agriculture. Awards and recognition followed, but for Li Wei, the greatest reward was seeing his village prosper. Farmers once burdened by uncertainty now harvested bountiful crops with confidence, their livelihoods secured by the union of tradition and modernity.

Through Li Wei's dedication and the collaborative efforts of scientists and farmers alike, a new chapter was written in the annals of rural China - one where the landscape was painted not just with green fields, but with hope and possibility for generations to come.

奉献的丰收

在中国农村的心脏地带，一望无际的田野中，李伟站在那里，成为农业发展中奉献与进步的象征。他生于一个小村庄，那里农耕不仅是一种生计，更是一种生活方式，李伟从小就与这片土地建立了深厚的情感联系。

年幼时，他见证了父母和邻里们辛勤劳作，使用代代相传的传统方法耕种土地。然而，李伟心中一直怀揣着一个梦想——将他们的劳动转化为更高效、更富产的结果。

在求知欲望和对农业科技的热情驱使下，李伟不畏艰难，攻读农业科学。他的求学之路并不轻松，离开熟悉的村庄，忍受教育求知过程中的各种困难，挑战传统农业智慧。

多年后，凭借着学位和远见，李伟以一个不同寻常的农民身份回到家乡。他投身于研究之中，与科学家和专家们合作，利用技术力量来推动乡村发展。

他的突破性进展始于精准农业技术的引入。借助无人机和卫星成像技术，李伟彻底改变了农作物管理的方式。农民们不再仅仅依赖天气模式和传统智慧，而是能够基于数据做出决策，优化产量，减少环境影响。

然而，李伟的贡献远不止于技术革新。他成为了可持续农业实践的倡导者，推动有机种植方法，保护土壤健康和生物多样性。他的努力不仅提升了农业生产的效率，更让农民们看到了他们辛勤劳作的成果转化为实实在在的收获。

随着季节的更替，李伟的名字在中国农业界逐渐成为创新和进步的象征。奖项和荣誉接连而来，然而对李伟而言，最大的奖赏是看到家乡的繁荣。曾经因不确定性而担忧的农民，现在充满信心地收获着丰盈的庄稼，他们的生计因传统与现代的结合而得以保障。

通过李伟的奉献和科学家与农民们的共同努力，中国农村写下了新的篇章——这不仅仅是绿色田野的画卷，更是未来希望和可能性的图景。

In fields of sweat, where passion burns,
A harvest blooms, for which one yearns.
No golden grain, nor fruit so sweet,
But dreams achieved, a victory complete.

With dedication, sown like seed,
Each day a task, a planted creed.
Through trials faced, and doubts that gnaw,
The roots of purpose hold us raw.

The sun, a witness, watches rise,
The patient care, the teary eyes.
For dedication's flame, though small,
Can light the path, and conquer all.

And when the harvest moon ascends,

The fruits of labor, joy transcends.
A heart fulfilled, a spirit strong,
The sweetest song, where we belong.

So let us raise a grateful hand,
For dedication's steadfast stand.
For in its toil, and endless fight,
We reap the harvest, bathed in light.

在汗水浇灌的田野，满腔热忱熊熊燃烧，
丰收盛景绽放，那是梦想的渴望。
并非金色谷粒，也非甜美果实，
而是实现的梦想，完美胜利的果实。

奉献为种，播撒心田，
每一天都是任务，种下的信念。
面对考验，战胜疑虑的折磨，
执着的根基让我们保持质朴。

太阳见证着日出，
辛勤付出，泪水盈眶。
奉献的火焰虽小，
却能照亮道路，征服一切。

当收获之月升起，
辛勤劳动的果实，喜悦超越一切。
心满意足，精神强健，
最甜蜜的歌谣，属于我们归属的地方。

让我们抬起感恩的手，
为奉献的坚定伫立欢呼。
因为在辛勤耕耘和无尽的奋斗中，
我们收获丰收，沐浴在光辉之中。

The Blossoming of Agricultural Intelligence

In the heart of rural China, nestled between verdant fields and under the expansive sky, Li Wei stood as a pioneer. His vision, grounded in both technological prowess and a deep-rooted love for the land, would forever change the landscape of agriculture.

Li Wei was not just an innovator; he was the architect behind China's agricultural expert systems and intelligent technologies. His journey began in the quiet village where he was born, where the rhythm of seasons dictated life. Growing up amidst rice paddies and orchards, he developed a profound respect for the farmers toiling under the sun.

Driven by a relentless curiosity and a passion to bridge the gap between tradition and modernity, Li Wei pursued studies in agricultural science and computer engineering. It was during his doctoral research that he envisioned a future where artificial intelligence could transform farming practices, making them more efficient and sustainable.

With unwavering determination, Li Wei pioneered the development of agricultural expert systems. These systems integrated data analytics, machine learning, and expert knowledge to provide farmers with real-time insights and recommendations. From crop management to pest control, every aspect of farming could now benefit from precision technology.

The road was not without challenges. Funding was scarce, and skepticism about technology's role in traditional agriculture ran deep. Yet, Li Wei persisted, collaborating with local farmers and demonstrating the tangible benefits of his innovations. Slowly, perceptions shifted, and his work gained recognition as a beacon of technological advancement in rural development.

As his systems spread across the countryside, transforming farms into hubs of efficiency and sustainability, Li Wei remained grounded in his mission. He believed in technology not as a replacement for traditional wisdom but as a complement—a tool to empower farmers and safeguard their livelihoods.

Years passed, and Li Wei's legacy grew. His name became synonymous with progress in agricultural technology, celebrated not only in China but also internationally. Awards and accolades followed, but for Li Wei, the greatest reward was seeing fields flourish and farmers thrive.

Reflecting on his journey, Li Wei often returned to his village, where he would quietly walk through fields he once played in as a child. The air was filled with the hum of machinery and the rustle of leaves—a testament to the harmony he had sought to achieve between nature and innovation.

Today, as China's high-tech agriculture blooms like a rare flower, Li Wei's pioneering spirit continues to inspire a new generation of innovators. His legacy stands as a reminder that with dedication and vision, even the most improbable dreams can take root and flourish.

农业智能的开花

在中国农村的心脏地带，李伟站在先锋的位置。他的愿景不仅根植于技术实力，还深深植根于对土地的热爱，这将永远改变农业的面貌。

李伟不仅是一位创新者，更是中国农业专家系统和智能技术的建筑师。他的旅程始于他出生的那个宁静的村庄，那里四季轮回主宰着生活。在稻田和果园中长大，他对在阳光下辛勤劳作的农民们养成了深厚的敬意。

在不懈的好奇心和架桥传统与现代之间的热情推动下，李伟攻读农业科学和计算机工程学。正是在他的博士研究期间，他构想了一个未来，在这个未来中，人工智能可以改变农业实践，使其更加高效和可持续。

怀着坚定的决心，李伟开创了农业专家系统的发展。这些系统整合了数据分析、机器学习和专家知识，为农民提供实时的见解和建议。从作物管理到病虫害控制，农业的每个方面现在都可以受益于精密技术。

道路并不是没有挑战的。资金稀缺，对技术在传统农业中角色的怀疑深入人心。然而，李伟坚持不懈，与当地农民合作，展示他的创新带来的实际好处。慢慢地，人们的看法发生了转变，他的工作得到了认可，成为农村发展中技术进步的象征。

随着他的系统在乡村传播，将农场转变为高效和可持续性的中心，李伟仍然致力于自己的使命。他相信技术不是传统智慧的替代品，而是一种补充——一种赋予农民力量和保护他们生计的工具。

岁月流逝，李伟的遗产日益增长。他的名字不仅在中国，还在国际上成为农业技术进步的代名词。奖项和荣誉接踵而至，但对李伟来说，最大的奖励是看到田野蓬勃发展，农民兴旺发达。

回顾自己的旅程，李伟常常回到他的村庄，静静地穿行在他童年玩耍过的田野中。空气中充满了机器的嗡鸣声和叶子的沙沙声——这是他寻求实现自然与创新和谐共生的证明。

今天，随着中国高科技农业如一朵稀世花朵般绽放，李伟的先锋精神继续激励着新一代创新者。他的遗产是一个提醒，即凭借奉献和远见，即使最不可思议的梦想也能生根发芽，蓬勃生长。

Where earth meets sky, a silent hum,
A verdant dance, the seeds succumb.
No farmer's call, no calloused hand,
But minds of code, across the land.

The Blossoming of Agricultural Intelligence,
A web of wisdom, a verdant renaissance.
Sensors whisper, data flows,
The land's secrets, knowledge grows.

Algorithms dance, a silent ballet,
Optimizing fields, come what may.
Yields maximized, with precision keen,
A greener future, on a digital screen.

From drought to deluge, the system sees,
Adjusting flows, with digital ease.
Pests and diseases, under its gaze,
Targeted solutions, for healthier days.

But fertile fields need more than code,
The human touch, upon the road.
A symphony of knowledge, hand in hand,
Man and machine, for a promised land.

So let us raise a grateful eye,
To blooming fields, that reach the sky.
For in this dance, of science and soul,
A future harvest, makes us whole.

沃野连天，静谧低吟，
青翠摇曳，种子沉眠。
非农夫吆喝，非老茧手掌，
代码思维，遍布疆场。

农业智能悄然绽放，
智慧织网，焕发荣光。
传感器轻语，数据流淌，
大地奥秘，知识激荡。

算法起舞，无声芭蕾，
优化田畴，无惧天灾。

产量精准，步步攀升，
数字屏幕，映照未来欣荣。

旱涝无忧，系统洞悉，
数字调节，滴水皆惜。
虫害病魔，无处遁形，
精准方案，迎来健康。

沃野丰饶，岂止代码，
需有人心，携手同行。
知识交响，携手共进，
人机协作，共赴盛景。

让我们满怀感恩，仰望天际，
朵朵绽放的田野，直指苍穹。
科技与灵魂的舞蹈，奏响乐章，
未来丰收，成就圆满梦想。

Wisdom Fields

In the rolling hills of rural China, where the rhythms of farming life have endured for centuries, a new dawn was breaking. The arrival of the Agricultural Expert System heralded a technological revolution in agriculture. Developed under the prestigious "National 863 Program," this computer artificial intelligence system aimed to empower farmers with cutting-edge agricultural techniques tailored to local needs.

In a small village nestled between terraced fields, Liang Wei, a seasoned farmer known for his resilience and innovation, attended a community meeting where the village chief unveiled the new system. Liang Wei, intrigued yet skeptical of modern technology, listened intently as the system's capabilities were explained. It promised to provide tailored advice on crop rotation, pest management, soil health, and weather forecasts—all crucial elements for successful farming in their region.

Over the weeks that followed, Liang Wei observed as younger farmers eagerly embraced the new technology. They accessed the system through their smartphones, receiving real-time recommendations and updates. Initially hesitant, Liang Wei eventually decided to give it a try, curious about how it could improve his harvest.

One morning, as dawn painted the sky in hues of pink and gold, Liang Wei sat in his modest farmhouse, tapping away on his old smartphone. He navigated through the system, entering data about his fields, the crops he planted, and the challenges he faced. Within seconds, the system analyzed the information and presented him with a comprehensive plan for the upcoming planting season.

With newfound optimism, Liang Wei followed the system's recommendations diligently. He adjusted his irrigation schedule, implemented organic pest control methods suggested by the system, and monitored soil nutrients more effectively. As the months passed, his fields flourished with healthier crops that fetched better prices at the market.

Word spread quickly through the village and neighboring communities. Farmers who had once been skeptical now sought Liang Wei's advice on using the Agricultural Expert System. Village gatherings buzzed with discussions on maximizing yields and sustainable farming practices. The once-silent smartphones became indispensable tools for every farmer, connecting them to a wealth of knowledge that transformed their traditional practices.

As harvest time approached, Liang Wei stood proudly amidst his abundant fields. The sun bathed the golden wheat in a warm glow, a testament to the harmony between age-old wisdom and modern innovation. With a heart full of gratitude, Liang Wei reflected on how the Agricultural Expert System not only improved his livelihood but also strengthened the bond among farmers in their shared pursuit of agricultural excellence.

In the quiet of the evening, as he gazed at the distant mountains silhouetted against the setting sun, Liang Wei felt a profound sense of optimism for the future of farming in China. The fields whispered tales of resilience and adaptation, where the seeds of tradition bloomed alongside the promise of technological advancement—a testament to the enduring spirit of those who toil the land.

This story explores the intersection of tradition and technology in agriculture, showcasing how advancements like the Agricultural Expert System can empower rural communities while honoring their agricultural heritage.

智慧之田

在中国农村起伏的丘陵地带，农耕生活的节奏已经延续了数百年，一个新的黎明正在到来。农业专家系统的出现标志着农业领域的技术革命。这一系统是在著名的"国家863计划"下开发的，旨在为农民提供针对地方需求量身定制的先进农业技术，以提升农业生产的效率和质量。

在一座梯田间的小村庄里，梁伟是一位以其坚韧和创新精神闻名的老农民。村长在一个社区会议上揭开了新系统的面纱。梁伟对现代技术既好奇又持怀疑态度，但他还是认真地听着系统功能的介绍。系统承诺为农民提供有关轮作种植、病虫害管理、土壤健康和天气预报等方面的个性化建议，这些对于当地农业的成功至关重要。

随着接下来的几周，梁伟看到年轻农民们迫不及待地接受了这一新技术。他们通过智能手机访问系统，即时获取建议和更新。起初有些犹豫的梁伟最终决定尝试一下，他想知道这种技术如何能够改善他的农作物收成。

一个清晨，当黎明将天空染成粉红色和金色时，梁伟坐在他朴素的农舍里，用他的老旧智能手机轻击着屏幕。他在系统中输入了关于他的田地、种植的作物以及他面临的挑战的数据。几秒钟后，系统分析了信息，为他提供了即将到来的种植季节的全面计划。

怀着新的乐观态度，梁伟始终如一地遵循系统的建议。他调整了灌溉时间表，采用系统建议的有机害虫控制方法，并更有效地监测土壤营养。随着时间的推移，他的田地里长出了更加健康的作物，这些作物在市场上卖得更好。

消息迅速传播到村庄和周边社区。曾经持怀疑态度的农民们现在纷纷向梁伟请教如何使用农业专家系统。村庄里的聚会上充满了关于如何最大化产量和可持续农业实践的讨论。一度沉默的智能手机成为每位农民的必不可少的工具，将他们与转变传统实践的丰富知识连接起来。

随着丰收的临近，梁伟自豪地站在他丰盈的田地中。太阳将金色的麦田染上温暖的光辉，这是传统智慧与现代创新之间和谐共处的见证。怀着感激之心，梁伟深深体会到农业专家系统不仅改善了他的生计，还在农民们共同追求农业卓越的道路上增强了他们之间的联系。

在夜幕降临时，当他凝视着远处山峦在夕阳映衬下的轮廓时，梁伟对中国农业的未来充满了乐观。田野间传来强烈的韵味，那里播种着传统的坚韧和现代技术进步的种子——这是那些辛勤耕耘土地的人们不懈精神的真实写照。

这个故事探讨了传统与技术在农业中的交汇，展示了农业专家系统如何在尊重农村传统的同时，赋予农民们技术上的力量，提升他们的农业生产水平。

In fields of thought, where wisdom grows,
No farmer sows, no harvest shows.
But seeds of truth, with care are spread,
By minds that learn, by lessons read.

The fertile ground, experience paved,
With failures tilled, and lessons saved.
Through trials weathered, doubts dispersed,
Knowledge takes root, a quench for thirst.

The sun of reason, bright and bold,
Illuminates these fields of gold.
With open minds, and hearts set free,
We glean the wisdom, endlessly.

The gentle rain of curiosity falls,
Nurturing questions, breaking walls.
For in the quest for deeper thought,
New understanding can be brought.

These fields of wisdom, vast and wide,
Where minds connect, from side to side.
With open dialogue, knowledge shared,
A tapestry of truth, with threads repaired.

So let us tend these fields with grace,
Where wisdom's bounty fills the space.
For in this growth, a future lies,
With minds enlightened, reaching for the skies.

思绪的田野，智慧生长，
无需农夫播种，亦无丰收景象。
但真理的种子，细心撒播，
学习的头脑，阅读的 lessons（教训）。

肥沃的土地，由经验铺就，
失败耕耘，教训珍藏。
历经磨难，疑惑消散，
知识扎根，解渴的甘泉。

理性的太阳，明亮而勇敢，
照耀着这些金色的田野。
思想开放，心灵自由，
我们无止境地汲取智慧。

好奇心化作轻柔的雨滴落下，
滋养疑问，打破藩篱。
因为在探索更深层次思想的征途上，
新的理解可以被带来。

这些 vast（辽阔的） and wide（宽广的） 智慧田野，
思想在此连接，心意相通。
开放的对话，分享知识，
修补真理的织锦。

让我们优雅地照料这些田野，
让智慧的恩赐填满空间。
因为在这片成长中，蕴藏着未来，
思想启迪，触摸天空。

The Green Symphony of Innovation

In the vibrant and hopeful green world, Li Wei plays the role of a guardian of agriculture. Through the seasons, with the wind and rain, he collaborates closely with agricultural experts, using scientific tools at his disposal to continuously enhance development and innovation tailored to China's agricultural conditions. Over more than thirty years of innovation, dedication, and perseverance, he orchestrates a spiritual anthem of agricultural technology.

Li Wei, born in a rural area, harbored a deep respect and love for every inch of farmland from a young age. Determined to transform Chinese agriculture, he immersed himself in agricultural technology research from university onwards, conducting field research and engaging directly with farmers to understand their practical needs.

After years of research and practice, Li Wei developed his own philosophy: to enhance agricultural productivity through technological means, protect the ecological environment of farmland, and achieve sustainable agricultural development. Leading a team, he developed a series of smart agricultural machinery and management systems that effectively addressed various challenges in cultivation, such as precision fertilization, smart irrigation, and pest control.

Li Wei's innovations did not stop there. He actively promoted agricultural technology knowledge, establishing close cooperation with local governments and agricultural cooperatives. Through training and demonstrations, he enabled more farmers to master advanced planting techniques, thereby improving their income and quality of life. His efforts not only transformed local agricultural production methods but also brought hope and new dreams to farmers.

Under Li Wei's leadership, this world of hope and dreams in green continues to embrace new challenges and opportunities. Each passing season, as crops thrive under their wisdom and technology, Li Wei feels immense satisfaction and pride. He knows that the path of smart agricultural development he has pioneered is not just a technological innovation but also a responsibility and commitment to the future of Chinese agriculture.

With over thirty years of steadfast dedication and hard work, Li Wei has truly become a guardian of agriculture. Through his wisdom and sweat, he orchestrates a spiritual anthem of agricultural technology, contributing his part to the modernization of Chinese agriculture.

在那精彩纷呈、充满希望与梦想的绿色世界里，李伟扮演的是一名农业"护航者"的身份。春去秋来，化风润雨，他结合中国国情，和农业专家紧密合作，用手中掌握的科学利器，不断完善发展创新，走出了一条我国农业智能工程独具特色的发展道路。他用三十多年的创新、奋斗和坚守，奏响了一曲来自农业科技的精神之歌。

李伟，一位生于乡村的农业科技专家，从小就对农田里的每一寸土地充满了敬畏和热爱。年轻时，他立志要改变中国农业的面貌，让每一片农田都能释放出最大的生产力。他从大学开始就投身于农业科技研究，深入实地调研，与农民交流，了解他们的实际需求。

经过多年的研究和实践，李伟逐渐形成了自己的理念：通过科技手段提升农业生产效率，保护农田生态环境，实现农业可持续发展。他带领团队研发了一系列智能农机设备和农业管理系统，有效地解决了种植过程中的诸多难题，比如精准施肥、智能灌溉、病虫害防治等。

李伟的创新并没有止步于此。他积极推广农业科技知识，与地方政府和农业合作社建立起紧密的合作关系。他通过培训和示范，让更多的农民掌握先进的种植技术，提高了他们的收益和生活质量。他的努力不仅改变了当地的农业生产模式，还为农民们带来了希望和新的梦想。

在李伟的带领下，这片充满希望与梦想的绿色世界，不断迎接着新的挑战和机遇。每当春去秋来，当农作物在他们的智慧与技术下茁壮成长，李伟都感到无比的满足和骄傲。他知道，自己走出的这条智能农业发展道路，不仅是一种科技创新，更是对中国农业未来的一种责任和担当。

三十多年的坚守和奋斗，让李伟成为了一名真正的农业"护航者"。他用自己的智慧和汗水，奏响了一曲来自农业科技的精神之歌，为中国农业的现代化进程贡献了自己的一份力量。

A verdant stage, where nature hums,
A symphony of progress drums.
No windblown reeds, nor strings of gold,
But minds alight, a story told.

The Green Symphony of Innovation,
A verdant choir of transformation.
Ideas sprout, like seedlings green,
Nurtured by dreams, a vibrant scene.

Sustainable notes, a gentle breeze,
Renewable power, rustling through the trees.
Technology's touch, a digital score,
Efficiency's whispers, wanting more.

Collaboration, a harmonious blend,
Sharing knowledge, until the very end.
From lab to field, a melody flows,
Where nature thrives, as knowledge grows.

Challenges rise, a discordant sound,
But innovation's resolve, on fertile ground.
With purpose clear, the music swells,
A symphony of hope, where progress dwells.

So let us listen, with hearts alight,
To the Green Symphony, taking flight.

For in this dance, of nature's embrace,
A greener future, finds its rightful place.

青翠舞台，自然低吟，
创新交响，奏响奋进。
非芦苇轻摇，非金色琴弦，
而是思想迸发，故事传扬。

绿色创新交响曲，
绿色合唱，奏响蜕变。
创意如苗，绿意盎然，
梦想滋养，生机勃勃。

可持续音符，如轻柔春风，
可再生能源，沙沙穿过树梢。
科技轻触，化作数字乐谱，
高效低吟，渴望更多。

协作共奏，和谐交融，
分享知识，直到最后。
从实验室到田野，旋律流动，
自然繁茂，知识增长。

挑战升起，音符杂乱，
但创新决心，沃土扎根。
目标明确，音乐澎湃，
希望交响，奏响未来。

让我们满怀热情，聆听乐章，
绿色交响曲，振翅高翔。
在大自然的拥抱中起舞，
更绿的未来，找到应有之地。

Fields of Insight

Professor Li Wei stood at the podium, bathed in the glare of cameras and the admiration of colleagues. His achievements in agricultural informatics had garnered international acclaim, yet his journey to this pinnacle was unconventional.

Sixteen years prior, fresh out of university, Li Wei embarked on a research career not in agriculture, but in industrial automation and computer technology. His path diverged sharply from his peers who pursued more traditional agricultural sciences. While others plowed fields, he navigated circuits and algorithms, mastering the intricacies of automation and control systems.

At first, his choice puzzled many. Why would a brilliant mind, destined for agricultural greatness, delve into the complexities of industrial processes? Li Wei's vision, however, transcended the immediate. He believed that modernizing agriculture required more than traditional agronomy; it demanded cutting-edge technology and innovative approaches.

His breakthrough came when he applied his expertise in automation to agricultural systems. By integrating advanced control algorithms with data analytics, Li Wei revolutionized precision farming. His systems optimized irrigation, minimized pesticide use, and maximized crop yields with unprecedented efficiency. Farmers who once doubted the relevance of technology in their fields now embraced Li Wei's innovations, transforming their practices and livelihoods.

As recognition poured in—a national contribution award, accolades from international conferences, fellowship in prestigious scientific societies—Li Wei remained grounded. He never forgot his unconventional beginnings, nor the skepticism he faced. Each accolade, to him, was not just personal triumph but a testament to the power of interdisciplinary thinking and perseverance.

Today, Professor Li Wei continues to push boundaries, exploring new frontiers where technology meets agriculture. His journey from industrial automation to agricultural informatics serves as a beacon of inspiration, reminding us that true innovation often emerges from unexpected intersections.

In the realm of agricultural sciences, Li Wei's name now shines brightly—a testament to the transformative potential of daring to forge new paths where none existed before.

This story celebrates Professor Li Wei's journey from industrial automation to agricultural informatics, highlighting his unconventional approach and the significant impact of his interdisciplinary work on modern agriculture.

洞察之域

李伟教授站在讲台前，身处摄像机的聚光灯和同事们的崇敬之中。他在农业信息学科领域的成就获得了国际认可，然而他通往这个巅峰的道路却是不寻常的。

十六年前，刚刚大学毕业的李伟选择了一个与众不同的研究方向，他并没有直接投身于农业领域，而是选择了工业自动化和计算机技术。他的选择与那些选择传统农学科的同龄人形成了鲜明对比。当其他人在田间劳作时，他却在电路和算法的世界里探索，精通自动控制系统的复杂技术。

最初，他的选择让很多人感到困惑。一个天赋出众、注定要在农业领域大放异彩的智慧，为何要沉迷于工业流程的复杂之中？然而，李伟的眼界超越了当下，他坚信现代化农业需要的不仅仅是传统的农学知识，更需要尖端技术和创新的方法。

他的突破来自于将工业自动化的专业知识应用到农业系统中。通过将先进的控制算法与数据分析结合，李伟彻底改变了精准农业的格局。他的系统优化了灌溉方案，最大程度减少了农药使用，并以前所未有的效率实现了农作物的最大产量。曾经怀疑技术在农业领域中应用价值的农民们，现在纷纷接受李伟的创新，改变着自己的耕作方式和生活。

随着荣誉的不断涌现——国家级有突出贡献专家、国际会议的赞誉、获得世界级科学学会的会士资格——李伟从未忘记他的不寻常起点和面对的怀疑。对他而言，每一个荣誉不仅仅是个人的胜利，更是跨学科思维和坚持不懈的力量的体现。

如今，李伟教授继续挑战极限，探索技术与农业相交汇的新领域。他从工业自动化到农业信息学科的旅程，成为了启发的典范，提醒我们真正的创新常常源自于意想不到的交汇点。

在农业科学的领域里，李伟的名字如今熠熠生辉——这不仅是个人成就的体现，更是敢于开拓新路的精神的象征。

In fields of insight, secrets sleep,
Beneath the surface, knowledge deep.
No farmer's plow, no harvest bright,
But hidden truths, unveiled by light.

The whispering wind of data flows,
Across the plains where wisdom grows.
Patterns emerge, like hidden veins,
Connecting concepts, easing strains.

With minds attuned, we learn to see,
The unseen forces, shaping reality.
The cause and effect, the silent tide,
That shifts the world, where fortunes hide.

From market trends to human thought,
The fields of insight wisdom sought.
Predictive whispers, soft and low,
Guiding actions, where the future's flow.

But fields of insight, vast and wide,
Can hold both shadows where truth may hide.
For data's grasp, though strong and keen,
Can miss the heart, the unseen scene.

So let us tread with cautious stride,
Through fields of insight, where shadows hide.
With wisdom's hand, and reason's might,
Unveil the truth, and guide us right.

洞察之田，秘密沉眠，
地表之下，蕴藏智慧渊泉。
非农夫耕犁，无丰收盛景，
唯有隐匿真理，待光揭明。

数据低语如风拂过，
智慧生长的田野辽阔。
脉络浮现，犹如隐蔽的血管，
连接概念，化解迷惘。

心智调谐，洞悉万物，
无形力量，塑造现实变换。
因果轮回，无声的浪潮，
推动世界，财富暗藏。

从市场趋势到人类思想，
洞察之田，智慧所求。
预测低语，轻柔婉转，
指引行动，未来流淌。

然而辽阔的洞察之田，
亦藏阴影，真理难辨。
数据掌控，虽强且锐利，
却可能错过人心，隐藏的意境。

因此让我们谨慎前行，
穿过洞察之田，拨开阴影。
以智慧之手，理性之光，
揭开真理，指引方向。

The Path of Innovation

In 1963, Li Wei graduated from the Department of Automation at the University of Science and Technology of China, becoming one of its first graduates. He was assigned to the East China Institute of Automation, Chinese Academy of Sciences, launching a career focused on automatic control and computer technology applications.

Over the next sixteen years, Li Wei immersed himself in extensive research in computer technology, laying a solid foundation for his future endeavors in the 1980s when he shifted his focus to agricultural expert systems and intelligent systems.

Entering the 1980s, China's agriculture faced new challenges and opportunities. Li Wei made the pivotal decision to combine his technical expertise with agriculture, dedicating himself to researching agricultural expert systems and intelligent technologies. This transition wasn't just a change in profession; it was a personal mission. He aimed to use his skills to reshape the trajectory of agricultural development.

Li Wei's new direction wasn't universally understood or supported. Some viewed it as a talented technologist "settling" for rural work, forsaking opportunities in urban areas for higher pay and prestige. Yet, Li Wei's passion for agriculture and vision for change kept him steadfast. He understood that only by integrating technology with practical needs could China truly modernize its agriculture.

As time progressed, Li Wei achieved remarkable success in agricultural intelligence. His designed agricultural expert systems helped farmers manage their fields more efficiently, increasing crop yields and improving living conditions for rural communities. His intelligent systems became a new hallmark for rural areas, enhancing productivity and offering technological convenience and hope to farmers.

Throughout his career, Li Wei witnessed rapid technological advancements and profound societal changes. He remained true to his initial aspirations and beliefs, undeterred by challenges, and wrote chapters of transformation in China's rural landscape with wisdom and courage. His journey wasn't just about technological exploration but also about fulfilling a personal mission, becoming a role model and inspiration for generations to come.

1963 年，李伟怀揣着满腔热忱和刚刚获得的自动控制理论专业学位，毕业于中国科技大学。他是该校第一届毕业生，被分配到中科院华东自动化研究所，开始了他在自动控制及计算机技术与应用领域的职业生涯。

最初的几年，李伟在研究所里埋头苦干，钻研计算机技术的种种奥秘。那个年代，计算机技术还处于萌芽阶段，每一次的成功都来之不易。李伟通过不懈的努力，逐渐成为领域内的专家，他的研究成果为自己未来的转型打下了坚实的基础。

进入八十年代，中国的农业正面临新的挑战和机遇。李伟决定将自己的专业知识与农业相结合，转而研究农业专家系统与智能系统。这一决定不仅是技术层面的转变，更是一种使命感的体现——他希望用自己的能力改变农业发展的轨迹。

李伟的新方向并不被所有人理解和支持。有人认为这是技术专家"屈就"于农村，放弃了在城市追求更高薪酬和声誉的机会。然而，李伟对于农业的热爱和改变的愿景让他坚定不移。他深知，只有将技术和实际需求结合，才能真正推动中国农业的现代化进程。

随着时间的推移，李伟在农业智能化领域取得了令人瞩目的成就。他设计的农业专家系统，帮助农民们更高效地管理农田，增加了农作物的产量，改善了农民的生活条件。他的智能系统成为农村的一张新名片，不仅提升了生产效率，也为农民们带来了技术上的便利和希望。

在李伟的职业生涯中，他经历了技术的飞速发展和社会的深刻变革。他始终坚持自己的初心和信念，不畏艰难，不惧挑战，用自己的智慧和勇气书写着一段段改变中国农村面貌的故事。他的经历不仅是技术探索的历程，更是对自己使命的践行，成为了一代人心中的典范和榜样。

A single thread, a dusty track,
Winding onward, turning back.
No paved highway, smooth and grand,
But choices whispered, hand in hand.

The Path, a journey ever-worn,
With lessons etched, at every turn.
Footsteps light, or heavy tread,
Each step unfolds, what lies ahead.

Through sun-drenched fields, or shadows deep,
The Path will guide, where secrets sleep.
With every rise, and every fall,
The Path unfolds, and conquers all.

Forged by dreams, and paved with doubt,
The Path winds on, with fervent shout.
A silent teacher, ever near,
Whispering courage, to quell our fear.

Where forks divide, and choices gleam,
The Path awaits, a silent dream.
For in the unknown, the heart takes flight,

And finds its way, in darkest night.

So let us walk, with purpose bold,
Embrace the Path, both young and old.
For in this journey, we shall find,
The truest self, and peace of mind.

一线尘径，蜿蜒曲折，
前行回望，诉说曾经。
非平坦大道，宽广壮丽，
而是耳语般的抉择，携手同行。

路径，历经磨损的旅程，
转折处刻画着教训。
脚步轻盈或是沉重，
每一步都揭示着前方。

穿过阳光普照的田野，或深邃的阴影，
路径将指引沉睡的秘密所在。
每一次上升，每一次下降，
路径延伸，征服一切。

由梦想铸造，由怀疑铺就，
路径蜿蜒，发出热切的呼喊。
一位无声的导师，始终陪伴，
低语着勇气，平息我们的恐惧。

岔路口出现，选择闪耀，
路径等待，一个无声的梦想。
因为在未知中，心将展翅高飞，
即使在最黑暗的夜晚，也能找到自己的道路。

让我们坚定地向前走，
拥抱道路，无论年轻还是年老。
因为在这段旅程中，我们将找到
最真实的自我，以及内心的平静。

All Mountains are low when you are in the height

In 1981, Li Wei, selected by the Institute of Intelligent Machinery at the Chinese Academy of Sciences in Hefei, embarked on a journey as a visiting scholar to the Computer Science Department of the University of Maryland, USA, to study artificial intelligence, pattern recognition, and image processing.

Li Wei was among the first batch of scholars to study abroad after China's reform and opening-up. His pride and sense of responsibility were palpable as he embarked on this rare opportunity, determined to learn diligently and contribute to his homeland.

"Artificial intelligence was a burgeoning field internationally, and back home, it was still in its infancy. For me, it was starting from ground zero," Li Wei reminisced.

The transition from the quiet laboratories of Hefei to the bustling campus of Maryland was overwhelming. Li Wei found himself amidst a diverse cohort of scholars from around the world, each bringing their unique perspectives to the field. Initially feeling like a small fish in a vast ocean, Li Wei soon adapted, fueled by his passion for learning and the support of his colleagues.

His days were consumed by rigorous study and research. He immersed himself in the intricacies of neural networks, algorithms, and the potential applications of AI in various fields. The collaborative atmosphere at Maryland encouraged him to think beyond boundaries, sparking ideas that blended Eastern philosophy with Western methodologies.

Outside the lab, Li Wei navigated the cultural nuances of American life. From casual conversations over coffee to weekend hikes in the nearby mountains, he cherished every interaction that broadened his worldview. The experience wasn't just about academic growth; it was a journey of personal discovery, forging friendships that transcended borders and languages.

As months turned into years, Li Wei's research flourished. His groundbreaking work on image recognition algorithms garnered attention both in the academic community and back home. Proudly, he shared his findings with colleagues in Hefei, bridging the gap between two worlds eager to harness the potential of AI.

"Returning home after my tenure was bittersweet. I had grown professionally and personally, but I carried with me a renewed sense of purpose," Li Wei reflected. Armed with newfound knowledge and a global network of collaborators, he continued to push the boundaries of AI research in China.

Decades later, as he stood overlooking the serene mountains of Hefei, Li Wei marveled at the journey that began with a single opportunity. His story, like the peaks that surrounded him, symbolized resilience, determination, and the enduring quest for knowledge.

"In the grand scheme of things," Li Wei mused, "every small step contributes to the larger landscape of progress."

This story captures Li Wei's transformative journey from China to the USA as a pioneering scholar in artificial intelligence, blending personal growth with professional achievements against the backdrop of cultural exchange and global collaboration.

一纵览群山小

1981 年，中国科学院合肥智能机械研究所选拔李伟作为访问学者前往美国马里兰大学计算机系，学习人工智能、模式识别与图像处理。

李伟是中国改革开放后第一批出国留学的学者之一。他充满自豪感和责任感，怀着对祖国的报效之心，迎接这难得的学习机会。

"国际上，人工智能是一门新兴学科，而国内刚刚起步。对我来说，这是从零开始的挑战。" 李伟怀念道。

从安静的合肥实验室到马里兰繁忙的校园，李伟面对来自世界各地的学者，每个人都带来了独特的视角。最初他在这个广阔的海洋中感到无所适从，但很快他适应了环境，坚定地投入到学习和研究中。

他的日子充满了严谨的学习和研究。他深入研究神经网络、算法以及人工智能在各个领域的潜在应用。马里兰的合作氛围鼓励他超越国界思考，激发了他将东方哲学与西方方法论相结合的创新思想。

实验室之外，李伟学会了理解和融入美国生活的文化细节。从咖啡间隙的随意对话到周末在附近山区的徒步旅行，每一个互动都拓宽了他的世界观。这段经历不仅仅是学术成长，更是个人发现之旅，建立了跨越国界和语言的友谊。

随着时间的推移，李伟的研究取得了长足进展。他在图像识别算法方面的突破性工作引起了学术界和国内的关注。他自豪地与合肥的同事分享自己的发现，架起了两个渴望利用人工智能潜力的世界之间的桥梁。

"结束访学回国后，我心情复杂。我在职业和个人方面都有了长足进步，但我也带着一种新的使命感。" 李伟深思熟虑地说道。凭借新获得的知识和全球合作者网络，他继续在中国推动人工智能研究的边界。

数十年后，站在合肥宁静的山脉上俯瞰，李伟惊叹于这段始于一个机会的旅程。他的故事，如周围的山峰一样，象征着坚韧、决心和对知识不懈追求。

"在宏大的蓝图中，每一小步都为进步的大格局贡献了力量。" 李伟沉思道。

这个故事记录了李伟作为人工智能先驱学者从中国到美国的转变之旅，融合了个人成长与专业成就，背景是文化交流和全球合作的背景。

Upon the peak, where eagles soar,
The world unfolds, forevermore.
No towering giants, peaks so grand,
But landscapes vast, at my command.

A panorama painted wide,
Where rivers dance, and mountains hide.
Forests whisper, secrets deep,
As clouds drift by, in slumbered sleep.

The world below, a tapestry,
Of colors rich, in harmony.
Villages nestled, fields of green,
A vibrant scene, a tranquil dream.

From lofty heights, the soul takes flight,
Embracing vastness, bathed in light.
Perceptions shift, horizons clear,
In this grand view, all doubts disappear.

So let us climb, with hearts ablaze,
To mountaintops, where wisdom stays.
For in this view, we truly see,
The boundless world, and all that's free.

登顶望远，鹰击长空，
寰宇铺展，亘古无穷。
巨峰不再巍峨险峻，
万水千山，尽收眼底。

一幅辽阔的图景

广袤画卷，徐徐展开，
河流蜿蜒，山峦隐现。
森林低语，诉说秘藏，
云朵飘逸，沉睡轻扬。

下方世界，织锦般瑰丽，
色彩斑斓，和谐共存。
村落依偎，绿野辽阔，
生机勃勃，宁静安详。

高耸入云，心灵展翅，
拥抱浩瀚，沐浴光明。
认知转变，视野明晰，
在这壮丽景色中，所有疑虑烟消云散。

让我们满怀热情，奋力攀登，
抵达山巅，智慧驻留。
因为在这景色中，我们真正领悟，
无垠世界，自由永恒。

The Bomb Explosion

Li Wei had only recently arrived in the United States to pursue a master's degree in computer science at a renowned university. He was just an ordinary international student, full of curiosity and anticipation for life in a foreign land.

However, a tragedy soon changed everything. During an unexpected bomb explosion, one of his close friends tragically lost his life, and Li Wei himself was seriously injured. The incident shocked the entire campus and garnered widespread attention both domestically and internationally.

In his hospital room, Li Wei received a phone call from Vice Premier Fang Yi, who expressed profound concern for him and his family. Fang Yi also extended an invitation for Li Wei to return to China for better treatment and recuperation. This unexpected care deeply touched Li Wei, bringing tears to his eyes as he keenly felt the warmth and support of his "motherland."

Faced with Fang Yi's condolences and invitation, Li Wei felt an extraordinary determination well up within him. Despite not yet fully recovering physically, he firmly expressed his desire to stay in the United States to continue his studies and life. He believed that as a Chinese person, he had a greater responsibility and mission to shine for his country abroad and contribute to the advancement of science and technology.

As time passed, Li Wei not only successfully completed his studies but also achieved a series of accomplishments in the field of computer science. He always carried deep affection for his homeland, dedicating all his achievements to the land he loved so dearly.

This is a story of resilience and belonging—a young man's journey of overcoming setbacks in a foreign land, supported by the care and encouragement from his homeland, as he pursues his dreams and contributes to global technological progress.

李伟刚刚来到美国不久，正在一所知名大学攻读计算机科学硕士学位。他本是个平凡的留学生，对于异国他乡的生活充满了好奇和期待。

然而，一场悲剧改变了他的一切。在一次意外的炸弹爆炸中，他的一个好友不幸丧生，而他自己也在爆炸中受了重伤。这起事故震惊了整个校园，也引起了国内外的广泛关注。

在李伟病房里，时任国务院副总理方毅亲自打来电话，表达了对他和他家人的深切关心，同时邀请他回国接受更好的治疗和休养。这个突如其来的关怀让李伟感到无比温暖和感动，他热泪盈眶，深深感受到了"祖国"的力量和温暖。

面对方毅的慰问和邀请，李伟心中涌起了不同寻常的决心。尽管身体还未完全康复，他坚定地表示，无论遇到什么困难，他都希望留在美国继续学习和生活。他深信，自己作为一名中国人，肩负着更多责任和使命，要在国外为祖国争光，为科学技术发展贡献自己的力量。

随着时间的推移，李伟不仅顺利完成了学业，还在计算机科学领域取得了一系列的成就。他始终怀抱着对祖国深厚的感情，将自己的一切成就都献给了那片他热爱的土地。

这是一个关于坚强和归属的故事，一个年轻人在异国他乡遭遇挫折后，如何在祖国的关怀和支持下，继续追逐自己的梦想，并为世界科技的进步贡献自己的力量。

In the realm of chaos, where fury takes flight,
An explosion erupts, shattering the night.
A blinding flash, a deafening roar,
As destruction unfolds, forevermore.

The force unseen, a tempest unleashed,
Buildings crumble, their structures breached.
Debris rains down, a tempestuous shower,
As flames dance and swirl, with demonic power.

In the smoke-filled haze, figures emerge,
Their faces etched with terror and surge.
The wounded cry out, their voices so frail,
As cries for help pierce the anguished wail.

Amidst the wreckage, heroes arise,
Their courage unwavering, beneath darkened skies.
They search for the trapped, with hands strong and true,
Their selfless acts, a beacon anew.

In the aftermath, a silence descends,
As the weight of loss on each heart attends.
Families mourn, their loved ones now gone,
Their lives extinguished, too soon, too soon.

Yet amidst the sorrow, a spirit ignites,
A resilience that shines, like beacon lights.
For in the face of darkness, humanity stands,
United in grief, with helping hands.

From the ashes of ruin, hope will arise,
A testament to the strength that lies
Within the human spirit, unbroken and bold,
A story of courage, a tale to be told.

爆裂巨响，划破长夜，
狂怒肆虐，混沌笼罩。
刺目闪光，震耳欲聋，
摧毁一切，永无止息。

无形之力，暴风骤起，
楼宇坍塌，支离破碎。
碎屑如雨，倾盆而下，
烈焰狂舞，恶魔之力。

烟雾弥漫，身影浮现，
恐惧与惊骇刻画在脸庞。
伤者呻吟，声音微弱，
求救声声，划破悲鸣。

废墟之中，英雄崛起，
即使乌云密布，勇气依旧。
他们寻找受困者，双手坚定，
无私奉献，闪烁光芒。

余音袅袅，寂静降临，
沉重悲伤，压迫着每颗心。
家庭哀悼，亲人离去，
生命逝去，转瞬即逝。

然而悲伤之中，精神燃起，
希望如灯塔，照亮天际。
面对黑暗，人类携手并肩，
悲痛相连，伸出援手。

从废墟灰烬中，希望升起，
证明着人类精神的坚韧，
永不屈服，永不退缩，
勇气与故事，将代代相传。

Overcoming the Odds

In the dim light of the study room, Li Wei glanced at the clock on the wall. It was nearly midnight, but his resolve was unshaken. Surrounded by towering stacks of books and scattered research papers, he was fully immersed in his studies. The hum of the fluorescent lights overhead and the faint ticking of the clock were the only sounds breaking the silence.

Li Wei had always been ambitious, but his journey to this point had been anything but easy. He came from a small village in China, where educational opportunities were scarce. His parents had worked tirelessly to provide for him, believing that education was the key to a better life. With their support and his own determination, Li Wei had secured a scholarship to study in the United States, a land full of promise and opportunity.

However, life abroad was a stark contrast to his expectations. The academic environment was highly competitive, and the language barrier made it even more challenging. Li Wei often felt like he was drowning in a sea of information, struggling to keep up with his peers. The pressure was immense, and the fear of failure loomed large over him.

Despite these challenges, Li Wei was determined not to let his dreams slip away. He adopted a rigorous study schedule, waking up at dawn and studying late into the night. He tackled one project after another, each one more complex than the last. His relentless effort began to pay off; he completed five or six major projects and wrote several research papers. One of his papers was even accepted for presentation at an international conference, a remarkable achievement that garnered praise from all quarters.

"The experience of studying in the US has had a profound impact on my work back home," Li Wei reflected. "Beyond the academic foundation, I've gained significantly in terms of research methods, innovative thinking, perseverance, and my English skills. Starting from scratch in a completely new field and being able to present my paper at an international conference was a breakthrough in courage and a significant boost in my self-confidence."

Li Wei's accomplishments were not just academic. They represented a transformation in his character and outlook. He had learned to navigate a new culture, to think critically and creatively, and to communicate effectively in a language that was once foreign to him. His time in the US had honed his resilience and adaptability, traits that would serve him well in his future endeavors.

As he prepared to return to China, Li Wei felt a sense of pride and anticipation. He knew that the skills and experiences he had gained would be invaluable in his career. More importantly, he hoped to inspire others with his story, showing them that with determination and hard work, it was possible to overcome even the most daunting challenges.

In the quiet of the night, Li Wei closed his books and turned off the light. He stood by the window, looking out at the city skyline. The journey had been tough, but he had emerged stronger and more confident. As he gazed at the distant horizon, he felt ready to embrace the future, equipped with the knowledge and skills to make a meaningful impact.

克服重重困难

在昏暗的学习室里，李伟瞥了一眼墙上的钟。已接近午夜，但他的决心丝毫未动摇。周围堆满了高高的书堆和散乱的研究论文，他完全沉浸在学习中。头顶上荧光灯的嗡嗡声和时钟的轻轻滴答声是打破寂静的唯一声音。

李伟一直都很有抱负，但他的旅程却并不容易。他来自中国的一个小村庄，那里教育机会稀少。他的父母辛勤工作，努力供他上学，相信教育是通向更好生活的钥匙。在他们的支持和他自己的决心下，李伟获得了去美国留学的奖学金，这是一个充满希望和机遇的地方。

然而，国外的生活与他的期望大相径庭。学术环境高度竞争，语言障碍更是增添了难度。李伟常常觉得自己在信息的海洋中挣扎，努力跟上同学的步伐。压力巨大，失败的恐惧在他心头挥之不去。

尽管如此，李伟决心不让梦想溜走。他制定了严格的学习计划，黎明即起，学习至深夜。他一个接一个地完成课题，每个课题都比前一个更复杂。他的不懈努力开始有了回报；他完成了五六个重大项目，并撰写了数篇研究论文。其中一篇论文甚至被接受在国际会议上发表，这是一个了不起的成就，赢得了多方赞扬。

"留美生活对我回国后工作影响很大，"李伟反思道，"除了学术基础，在科研方法、创新思维、工作毅力和英语能力等方面，我都得到了显著提高。从零起步到能在国际会议上发表论文，确实是胆量的突破和自信心的阶跃性提高。"

李伟的成就不仅仅是学术上的，它们代表了他性格和观点的转变。他学会了在新文化中游刃有余，学会了批判性和创造性思维，并能有效地用曾经陌生的语言进行交流。在美国的经历磨砺了他的韧性和适应能力，这些特质在未来的事业中将大有裨益。

当他准备返回中国时，李伟感到自豪和期待。他知道自己所获得的技能和经验将在事业中发挥重要作用。更重要的是，他希望通过自己的故事激励他人，告诉他们，只要有决心和努力，即使是最艰难的挑战也可以克服。

在夜的静谧中，李伟合上书，关掉了灯。他站在窗前，眺望城市的天际线。旅途虽然艰辛，但他变得更强大、更自信。当他凝视远方的地平线时，感到自己已经准备好迎接未来，凭借所学知识和技能，创造有意义的影响。

Where shadows loom and burdens weigh,
A path unfurls, a challenging way.
Difficulties rise, like mountains steep,

But within us lies the will to leap.

Doubt whispers low, a chilling breeze,
"This path's too hard, find solace, please."
But courage calls, a steady drum,
"We'll rise above, we'll overcome!"

With each firm step, the ground takes hold,
Resilience blooms, a story told.
We learn from stumbles, dust ourselves off,
Forged in the fire, we're strong enough.

Help comes in hands, a reaching light,
A shared resolve, a guiding might.
Together we climb, a steadfast band,
Overcoming mountains, hand in hand.

Though trials test and tempests blow,
Hope's ember burns, a steady glow.
For with each challenge bravely faced,
We find the strength, the victory embraced.

So let us rise, and meet the fight,
With hearts ablaze, and spirits bright.
For difficulties, though they may loom,
Are stepping stones to conquer gloom.

阴影笼罩，重担压身，
道路蜿蜒，挑战在前。
困难矗立，如山峻峭，
但心中意志，渴望奋跃。

疑虑低语，寒风刺骨，
"道路艰险，何必执着？"
然而勇气呼唤，鼓声坚定，
"我们将超越，必将克服！"

每一步坚定，足迹踏实，
坚韧绽放，故事述说。
从跌倒中学习，掸去尘埃，
浴火重生，愈发强大。

援手相助，光芒闪耀，
共同决心，指引方向。
携手并肩，坚定向上，
跨越山峦，团结奋战。

即使考验重重，暴风雨袭，
希望之火，永不熄灭。
因为勇敢面对每一次挑战，
我们将找到力量，拥抱胜利。

让我们奋起，迎接战斗，
炽热之心，明亮的灵魂。
困难虽强，终将消散，
是通往光明之路的基石。

No Time to Waste, Serving the Country Starts Now

After returning to his homeland, Li Wei was eager to serve his country. He hoped to quickly apply the knowledge he had gained abroad in the field of robotics. However, not long after, he chose to research agricultural expert systems—a decision that seemed coincidental but was inevitable.

The story of this coincidence began during his studies in the United States. A few months before his return, one day, renowned Chinese-American professor Hua Yizu called him and urgently urged him to learn about expert systems, saying, "This will be very useful for China." For someone eager to serve his country, this seemed like a silent command, propelling him into a state of intense learning, attending lectures, and collecting materials.

Upon receiving the call, Li Wei was initially taken aback. Robotics had been his passion and focus throughout his academic career. The idea of diverting his attention to expert systems felt like an unexpected detour. Yet, Professor Hua's words resonated deeply with him. He couldn't shake off the feeling that there was a greater purpose behind this suggestion.

Driven by a sense of duty and curiosity, Li Wei immersed himself in the study of expert systems. He discovered that these systems had the potential to revolutionize various industries by simulating the decision-making abilities of human experts. The more he learned, the more he realized the vast applications and benefits these systems could bring to his homeland, particularly in the agricultural sector.

Agriculture had always been a critical part of China's economy and culture. Despite the rapid urbanization and industrialization, a significant portion of the population still relied on farming for their livelihood. Li Wei saw an opportunity to integrate modern technology with traditional farming practices to improve efficiency, productivity, and sustainability.

Upon his return to China, Li Wei was determined to put his newfound knowledge to use. He joined a research institute that focused on agricultural technology. His colleagues were initially skeptical about his shift from robotics to expert systems, but Li Wei's passion and conviction soon won them over.

He began by developing a prototype of an expert system tailored for Chinese farmers. This system could analyze soil conditions, weather patterns, and crop health to provide farmers with precise recommendations on planting, fertilizing, and harvesting. The goal was to empower farmers with the tools and knowledge to make informed decisions, ultimately improving their yields and livelihoods.

The initial trials of the expert system were met with great success. Farmers who used the system reported significant improvements in their crop quality and productivity. Word spread quickly, and soon, more farmers were eager to adopt this innovative technology.

Li Wei's work did not stop there. He collaborated with local governments and agricultural organizations to expand the reach of the expert system. Training programs were established to educate farmers on how to use the technology effectively. He also worked on integrating other technologies, such as drones and IoT devices, to enhance the capabilities of the expert system further.

As the agricultural expert system gained traction, Li Wei felt a profound sense of fulfillment. He realized that this was his true calling—to bridge the gap between advanced technology and traditional practices, and to make a tangible difference in the lives of his fellow countrymen.

Years later, reflecting on his journey, Li Wei understood that his decision to shift from robotics to agricultural expert systems was not a mere coincidence. It was a path that had been laid out for him, driven by his unwavering desire to serve his country. He had found his purpose in the radiant transformation of China's agricultural landscape, proving that there was indeed no time to waste when it came to the progress and prosperity of his homeland.

华丽转身：时光不能空耗，报国即刻出发

回国后，李伟报效祖国之心非常迫切，希望将国外学到的机器人研究方向赶快开展起来。但不久后，他却选择了研究农业专家系统，这似乎偶然，但确也是必然。

说起偶然，还得从他在美国留学时说起。当时离回国还有几个月，一天，著名华裔教授华怡祖打电话叫他赶快学习专家系统技术，说"对中国非常有用"。对急于报效祖国的他来说，这似乎是无声的命令在推动着他，让他迅速进入"紧张听课，收集资料"的学习状态。

接到电话后，李伟起初感到惊讶。机器人学一直是他学术生涯中的热情和焦点。将注意力转向专家系统的想法感觉像是一个意想不到的转折。然而，华教授的话在他心中深深共鸣。他无法摆脱这种感觉，这个建议背后有更大的目的。

出于责任感和好奇心的驱使，李伟投入到专家系统的学习中。他发现这些系统通过模拟人类专家的决策能力，能够彻底改变各个行业。他学习得越多，就越意识到这些系统可以给他的祖国带来的广泛应用和好处，尤其是在农业领域。

农业一直是中国经济和文化的重要组成部分。尽管快速的城市化和工业化，仍有相当一部分人口依赖农业为生。李伟看到了一个将现代技术与传统农业实践相结合的机会，以提高效率、生产力和可持续性。

回到中国后，李伟决心将新学到的知识付诸实践。他加入了一家专注于农业技术的研究所。他的同事们最初对他从机器人学转向专家系统持怀疑态度，但李伟的热情和信念很快赢得了他们的认可。

他首先开发了一个针对中国农民的专家系统原型。该系统可以分析土壤条件、天气模式和作物健康状况，为农民提供关于种植、施肥和收获的精确建议。目的是通过赋予农民工具和知识来做出明智的决策，最终提高他们的产量和生活水平。

专家系统的初步试验取得了巨大成功。使用该系统的农民报告称，他们的作物质量和生产力显著提高。消息很快传开，很快更多的农民渴望采用这一创新技术。

李伟的工作并没有就此止步。他与地方政府和农业组织合作，扩大专家系统的覆盖范围。建立了培训项目，教育农民如何有效使用这项技术。他还致力于整合其他技术，如无人机和物联网设备，以进一步增强专家系统的功能。

随着农业专家系统的普及，李伟感到一种深深的满足感。他意识到这才是他的真正使命——弥合先进技术与传统实践之间的差距，并在同胞的生活中做出切实的改变。

多年后，回顾自己的历程，李伟明白了，从机器人学转向农业专家系统的决定不仅仅是一个巧合。这是一条为他铺设的道路，驱动他无比坚定地报效祖国。他在中国农业景观的华丽转身中找到了自己的目标，证明了在祖国的进步和繁荣面前，确实没有时间可以空耗。

In service true, a heart ablaze,
For land we love, in countless ways.
No trumpet sounds, no banners fly,
But quiet pride, beneath the sky.

The soldier stands, on distant shore,
Defending peace, forevermore.
The teacher guides, with gentle hand,
Shaping young minds, for this fair land.

The farmer sows, with sweat and toil,
Nourishing the earth, on fertile soil.
The scientist probes, with endless quest,
For knowledge bright, to put to the test.

The artist paints, a vibrant hue,
The nation's soul, forever new.
The builder crafts, with steady hand,
A future strong, on solid land.

From every walk, from every stride,
A thread is woven, deep and wide.

A tapestry of purpose grand,
Serving the country, hand in hand.

For love of home, a fire bright,
Inspires us all, to do what's right.
In every act, however small,
We serve the nation, one and all.

So let us rise, with voices strong,
To sing of service, righting wrong.
For in this chorus, hearts entwined,
A stronger nation, we shall find.

忠诚之心，熊熊燃烧，
为挚爱国土，千千万万。
无需军号，无需旌旗，
唯有静默自豪，映衬天际。

战士远驻，异国他乡，
捍卫和平，世世代代。
教师引领，手把手足，
塑造幼苗，为这片沃土。

农夫辛勤，汗洒大地，
肥沃土地，五谷丰登。
科学家探索，孜孜不倦，
追求知识，勇于考验。

艺术家挥毫，色彩斑斓，
描绘国家，生生不息。
建筑工人，技艺精湛，
建造未来，稳固基石。

每一步脚印，每一个岗位，
汇成宽广织锦，生生不息。
宏伟目标的锦绣画卷，

携手奉献，服务国家。

爱国之火，熊熊燃烧，
激励着我们，做正直之事。
每一个行动，无论大小，
我们都是中华儿女，服务国家。

让我们扬起声音，同声歌唱，
为奉献而歌，匡扶正义。
心与心交织，合唱嘹亮，
我们将铸就更加强大的祖国。

Unexpected Seeds

Li Wei had always been fascinated by technology. Growing up, he devoured books on engineering, dreamed of building complex machines, and spent his nights tinkering with electronics. His hard work paid off, and he eventually secured a scholarship to study in the United States, where he dove into the burgeoning field of expert systems, a branch of artificial intelligence.

Upon his return to China, Li Wei found a position at a leading tech company. He was thriving, developing cutting-edge AI systems for industrial applications, but his work felt detached from the everyday lives of most people. While he loved his job, there was a nagging feeling that something was missing.

One day, at a technology conference in Beijing, Li Wei ran into an old friend from university, Zhang Jie, who now worked as the Director of Science and Technology at the Anhui Agricultural Research Institute. Over a cup of tea, they reminisced about their university days and the challenges they faced.

Zhang Jie casually mentioned the difficulties they were having in agriculture. "You know, Li Wei, the technology you learned in the U.S., could it be applied to our agriculture?" he asked, almost as an afterthought.

Li Wei chuckled, "Agriculture? Really? I never thought about that. Back in the day, none of us wanted anything to do with farming. We all aimed for engineering, medicine, anything but agriculture. It seemed so backward, so primitive compared to the industrial and military technologies we were drawn to."

Zhang Jie nodded in agreement, "I know. That's why we need minds like yours. Agriculture doesn't have to be backward. With the right technology, we could revolutionize it."

Li Wei went home that night, Zhang Jie's words echoing in his mind. The idea of using his expertise in AI to help farmers was intriguing. He began to research the current state of agricultural technology and realized that there was a significant gap that could be bridged with modern AI systems.

Over the next few months, Li Wei immersed himself in the world of agriculture. He visited farms, spoke with farmers, and learned about the unique challenges they faced. The more he learned, the more passionate he became about applying his knowledge to improve agricultural practices.

Li Wei proposed a project to his company to develop an AI-based expert system specifically for agriculture. His colleagues were skeptical at first. "Agriculture? Isn't that a bit... beneath us?" one of them asked.

Li Wei smiled, "Not at all. If we can make a difference in the lives of millions of farmers, isn't that worth pursuing?"

The company eventually agreed, and Li Wei led a team to develop an AI system that could analyze soil data, predict weather patterns, and provide real-time advice to farmers on when to plant, irrigate, and harvest their crops. The system also included pest and disease detection, offering solutions to combat issues before they became widespread.

The project faced numerous challenges, from integrating traditional farming knowledge with modern technology to convincing farmers to adopt the new system. But Li Wei persisted, driven by the potential impact on the agricultural sector.

One of the pilot sites for the project was a village in Anhui province. The farmers there were initially wary of the technology, but as they began to see the benefits—higher yields, healthier crops, and reduced costs—they embraced it wholeheartedly.

The success of the project caught the attention of agricultural experts and policymakers. Li Wei's system was soon being implemented in villages across China, transforming the way farming was done. The once reluctant engineer had become a pioneer in agricultural technology, proving that even the most unlikely paths could lead to significant and rewarding outcomes.

Reflecting on his journey, Li Wei realized that sometimes, the most impactful innovations come from unexpected opportunities and a willingness to explore beyond conventional boundaries. The accidental conversation with Zhang Jie had planted a seed in his mind, one that had grown into a thriving endeavor, changing the face of agriculture in China and beyond.

意外的种子

李伟一直对技术充满热情。从小，他就贪婪地阅读关于工程的书籍，梦想着制造复杂的机器，夜晚则花在电子设备的捣鼓上。他的努力得到了回报，最终获得了奖学金，前往美国深造，投身于新兴的专家系统领域，这是一种人工智能的分支。

回到中国后，李伟在一家领先的科技公司找到了工作。他在工业应用领域开发最前沿的人工智能系统，事业蒸蒸日上，但他的工作感觉与大多数人的日常生活脱节。尽管他热爱自己的工作，但总觉得缺少了什么。

一天，在北京的一次技术会议上，李伟遇到了大学时代的老朋友张杰，现在担任安徽农业科学院科技处长。在喝茶聊天时，他们回忆起大学时光和所面临的挑战。

张杰随口提到他们在农业中遇到的困难。"你知道吗，李伟，你在美国学到的技术，能不能用到我们农业上？"他几乎是随意地问了一句。

李伟笑了，"农业？真的？我从没想过这个。当年我们都不愿意接触农业。大家都想考工程、医学，什么都好，就是不想搞农业。农业看起来那么落后，相比工业和军事技术简直不值一提。"

张杰点了点头，"我知道。所以我们需要像你这样的头脑。农业不一定要落后。有了合适的技术，我们可以彻底改变它。"

那天晚上，李伟回到家，张杰的话在他脑海中回荡。将自己的专业知识应用于帮助农民的想法令人着迷。他开始研究农业技术的现状，并意识到存在一个可以用现代人工智能系统填补的巨大鸿沟。

接下来的几个月，李伟全身心投入到农业的世界。他参观了农场，与农民交谈，了解他们面临的独特挑战。他学得越多，就越对用他的知识改善农业实践充满热情。

李伟向公司提出了一个项目，开发一个专门用于农业的人工智能专家系统。他的同事们起初持怀疑态度。"农业？这不是有点……低吗？"其中一位问道。

李伟微笑着说，"一点也不。如果我们能改变数百万农民的生活，这难道不值得追求吗？"

公司最终同意了，李伟带领团队开发了一套人工智能系统，能够分析土壤数据、预测天气模式，并实时为农民提供种植、灌溉和收获的建议。系统还包括害虫和疾病检测，提供解决方案以在问题变得普遍之前进行防控。

项目面临着许多挑战，从将传统农业知识与现代技术相结合，到说服农民采用新系统。但李伟坚持了下来，驱动力来自于对农业部门潜在影响的热情。

该项目的一个试点地点是安徽省的一个村庄。那里的农民起初对技术持怀疑态度，但随着他们看到收益——更高的产量、更健康的作物和更低的成本——他们全心全意地接受了它。

项目的成功引起了农业专家和政策制定者的关注。李伟的系统很快在中国各地的村庄推广，改变了农业的方式。这个曾经不情愿的工程师成为了农业技术的先锋，证明了即使是最不可能的道路也能带来重要且有价值的成果。

回顾自己的旅程，李伟意识到，有时候，最有影响力的创新来自于意外的机遇和愿意探索常规界限之外的精神。与张杰的那次偶然对话在他的脑海中播下了一颗种子，这颗种子成长为一项蓬勃发展的事业，改变了中国乃至全球的农业面貌。

A pocket forgotten, a coat laid aside,
A silent stowaway, a journey to ride.
No gardener's hand, nor purposeful sow,

An unexpected seed, on the wind does it go.

On concrete it lands, a harsh, barren ground,
Yet hope perseveres, a strength unbound.
It cracks the pavement, with will to survive,
A tiny green shoot, where nothing thrived.

The city's embrace, a jungle of steel,
But the seedling persists, a determined appeal.
It reaches for sunlight, a sliver so thin,
A testament to life, where it can win.

Through cracks in the sidewalk, it pushes its way,
A splash of green, on a monotonous gray.
A symbol of resilience, a whisper so bold,
That beauty can bloom, even from stories untold.

The unexpected seed, a lesson unfolds,
Of tenacity's power, in a world that grows cold.
For even in darkness, a seed finds its light,
A reminder to fight, with all of our might.

So let us take heart, from this chance-planted thing,
And nurture the seeds, the dreams that we bring.
For even the unexpected, can blossom and grow,
If hope takes the lead, where the wild winds blow.

被遗忘的口袋，搁置的外套，
一颗沉默的种子，即将启航。
并非园丁之手，也非刻意播种，
一颗意外的种子，随风飘扬。

它落在水泥地上，一片荒芜之地，
但希望依然坚韧，力量无限。
它冲破路面，渴望生存，
一株幼小的嫩芽，在毫无生机处崛起。

城市的拥抱，钢铁的丛林，

然而幼苗坚强不屈，发出坚定的呼唤。
它向着阳光生长，一丝微弱的光线，
生命的证明，在任何可能的地方绽放。

穿过人行道的裂缝，它奋力向上，
一抹绿色，点缀单调的灰色。
一种坚韧的象征，一个大胆的低语，
即使是未知的故事，也能绽放美丽。

这颗意外的种子，揭示了一个道理，
在逐渐冷却的世界里，顽强不屈的力量。
即使在黑暗中，种子也能找到光明，
提醒我们全力以赴，为梦想而战。

因此，让我们从这个偶然播种的事物中汲取勇气，
培育种子，培育我们带来的梦想。
因为即使是意外，也能盛开和成长，
只要希望引领着我们，即使狂风肆虐。

A Beacon in the Fields

In the mid-1980s, Beijing was a hub of excitement and innovation. The Chinese Academy of Sciences, along with key government officials, was engaged in a series of crucial meetings. The goal: to formulate a high-tech development plan for China. The world was rapidly advancing technologically—America with its "Star Wars" program and Japan with its "Fifth Generation Computer" project. China faced the pressing question: What should our next step be?

Among the chosen few to participate in these discussions were two young visionaries. One of them was Li Wei, a brilliant mind freshly returned from studying abroad. The other was Ni Guangnan, who would later become the founder of Lenovo. Together, they attended numerous meetings that would lay the groundwork for the famous 863 Program, China's ambitious high-tech R&D initiative.

During one pivotal meeting, Li Wei approached the esteemed Wang Daheng, a luminary in the field. With fervor, he requested permission to apply the cutting-edge technology he had learned overseas to military projects. Wang Daheng, with a reassuring smile, replied, "Don't worry, it will happen soon!" This promise meant that Li Wei could have easily pursued high-precision projects in defense or industry under the 863 Program.

However, Li Wei's patriotic zeal and his disdain for wasting precious time drove him to look beyond the immediate horizon. He couldn't wait for the gears of bureaucracy to turn. Instead, he proactively directed his energy towards researching applications in other areas. He sought to make an immediate impact, not wanting to let any moment slip by unutilized.

During the mid-1980s, China experienced a surge of interest in expert systems, particularly in the field of medical expert systems. However, Li Wei perceived a different, yet equally vital, application: agriculture. He envisioned expert systems revolutionizing the agricultural sector, enhancing productivity and efficiency.

Li Wei's vision was clear. He saw the potential for expert systems to analyze vast amounts of data and provide precise recommendations to farmers, ultimately boosting crop yields and ensuring food security for the nation. This foresight led him to focus on agricultural development, a decision that would define his career and legacy.

Driven by his passion and foresight, Li Wei embarked on a new journey. He collaborated with agricultural scientists and technologists, delving deep into the intricacies of farming. He developed systems that could predict pest outbreaks, optimize irrigation schedules, and recommend the best crop varieties for different regions.

Li Wei's work quickly gained recognition. Farmers across China began to adopt these expert systems, and the results were astounding. Crop yields increased, farming became more efficient, and the lives of countless farmers improved. Li Wei's contributions were not just technological; they were transformative for rural China.

Years later, at a grand ceremony honoring the contributors to China's technological advancement, Li Wei stood alongside his peers, including Ni Guangnan. As he received his award, he reflected on his journey. He had chosen a path less glamorous but profoundly impactful. His decision to focus on agriculture had helped secure China's food supply and uplifted millions of lives.

In his acceptance speech, Li Wei humbly stated, "Innovation is not just about advancing technology; it's about improving lives. I'm grateful for the opportunity to serve my country in the fields, where the real seeds of our future are sown."

His words resonated deeply with the audience, a reminder that true patriotism is not just about grand projects but about making tangible differences in people's lives. Li Wei's legacy became a testament to the power of vision, dedication, and the unwavering desire to serve one's country.

田野中的灯塔

20 世纪 80 年代中期，北京成为了兴奋与创新的中心。中国科学院与政府要员们正在进行一系列重要会议，目标是为中国制定高科技发展规划。世界正在迅速推进科技进步——美国有"星球大战"计划，日本有"第五代计算机"项目。中国面临着紧迫的问题：我们的下一步该怎么走？

在这些参与讨论的少数天才中，有两位年轻的远见卓识者。一位是刚从海外学习归来的李伟，另一位是后来联想的创始人倪光南。他们一起参加了无数次会议，这些会议奠定了后来著名的 863 计划的基础。

在一次关键会议上，李伟怀着极大的热情向著名的王大珩请求，能否将他在国外学到的尖端技术应用于军事项目。王大珩带着安抚的微笑回答道："你不要着急，快了！"这意味着李伟完全可以在 863 计划下，从事国防或工业领域的高精尖项目。

然而，李伟那种强烈的报效祖国的心情和珍惜宝贵时光的习性，使他无法等待官僚机器的缓慢运转。相反，他主动将精力投入到其他领域的研究中，希望立即产生影响，不想让任何时光白白流逝。

20 世纪 80 年代中期，中国曾经掀起了一股专家系统热，特别是在医学专家系统领域。然而，李伟看到了农业专家系统的巨大潜力和应用前景。他设想，专家系统可以通过分析大量数据，为农民提供精确的建议，最终提高作物产量，确保国家的粮食安全。

李伟的愿景十分明确。他看到了专家系统能够分析大量数据，为农民提供精准建议，最终提高作物产量，确保国家的粮食安全。这一远见让他选择了农业发展，并决定投身其中。

在激情和远见的驱动下，李伟开始了新的征程。他与农业科学家和技术专家合作，深入研究农业的复杂性，开发了能够预测害虫爆发、优化灌溉时间表以及推荐不同地区最佳作物品种的系统。

李伟的工作很快获得了认可。中国各地的农民开始采用这些专家系统，结果令人惊叹。作物产量增加，农业效率提高，数百万农民的生活得到了改善。李伟的贡献不仅仅是技术上的；它们对中国农村地区产生了深远的影响。

多年后，在一个表彰为中国科技进步做出贡献的盛大仪式上，李伟与包括倪光南在内的同行们一起站在了台上。当他接过奖项时，他回想起自己的旅程。他选择了一条不那么光彩但却深具影响力的道路。他专注于农业的发展，帮助保障了中国的粮食供应，改善了无数人的生活。

在他的获奖感言中，李伟谦逊地说道："创新不仅仅是技术的进步，更是生活的改善。我很感激能够有机会在田野中为国家服务，在那里种下了我们未来的真正种子。"

他的言辞深深打动了在场的观众，提醒大家真正的爱国主义不仅仅是宏大的项目，而是对人民生活产生的实际影响。李伟的遗产成为了远见、奉献以及不懈服务国家愿望的见证。

In fields of gold, where twilight dips,
A solitary beacon tips.
No flickering flame, no bonfire's glow,
But silent light, a guiding flow.

A Beacon in the Fields, it stands,
A watchful eye on fertile lands.
Across the plains, its message streams,
A promise bright, in moonlit beams.

With gentle hum, it whispers low,
Of knowledge sown, to help crops grow.
Soil conditions, it can assess,
And guide the farmer, with success.

Through drought and storm, its vigil kept,
A silent guardian, while others slept.
Alerts it sends, with timely chime,
Protecting harvests, beating time.

More than just light, this beacon brings,
The hope of science, on future wings.
For in its gaze, a promise gleams,
Of bountiful fields, and fruitful dreams.

So let us raise a grateful eye,
To the beacon's light, that paints the sky.
A silent hero, in the night,
Guiding farmers, to a future bright.

金色田野，暮色低垂，
孤傲的灯塔，高耸入云。
并非跳跃的火焰，也非篝火余晖，
而是无声的光芒，引领着航线。

田野中的灯塔，伫立不息，
守护着沃土的守望之眼。
穿越平原，它的信息如流淌，
明月照耀下，闪耀着明亮的承诺。

伴随着轻柔的嗡嗡声，它轻声低语，
播撒知识，帮助庄稼茁壮成长。
它能评估土壤状况，
指引农民走向成功。

经历干旱和风暴，它始终坚守，
当人们熟睡时，它默默守护。
及时发出警报，敲响钟声，
保护着丰收，把握着时间。

这盏灯塔不仅带来光明，
更带来科学的希望，翱翔于未来的羽翼上。
在它的注视下，一个承诺闪耀，
丰饶的田野，丰硕的梦想。

让我们满怀感激地仰望，
那盏灯塔的光芒，照亮天空。
夜晚的沉默英雄，
指引着农民走向光明未来。

A Spark in the Fields

Li Wei traveled to numerous places in his quest to explore potential agricultural applications, including breeding and animal husbandry. His journey was driven by curiosity and a desire to bring advanced agricultural techniques to his homeland. One fortuitous encounter brought him to Anhui Province Agricultural Research Institute, where he met Wu Wenrong, an expert in soil fertility who had spent years conducting scientific fertilization research in rural experimental sites.

Wu was a seasoned veteran of the fields, having dedicated his life to understanding the intricacies of soil and plant nutrition. In contrast, Li Wei had returned from the United States armed only with a handful of articles on the general applicability of expert systems, with scant knowledge of international agricultural research.

They faced significant challenges from the start. There were no assistants to help them, no funding to support their projects. Just the two of them, coming from entirely different fields, trying to communicate, share ideas, and collaborate. In the initial months, their discussions were often fruitless, as they struggled to find common ground or a starting point for their work.

Frustration began to set in as the months passed without any tangible progress. Their conversations were filled with theoretical debates and speculative ideas, with no clear direction or actionable plans. However, one day, as Li Wei was combing through research reports, he stumbled upon a summary report on a mortar black soil fertilizer experiment. Among the pages of data and analysis, a particular fertilizer effect equation caught his eye.

"This is it!" Li Wei nearly shouted, his excitement palpable. "This is where we can start!"

Wu looked over, intrigued by Li Wei's sudden burst of enthusiasm. As they delved into the report together, they realized that the equation provided a practical foundation they could build upon. It was a breakthrough moment, a spark that ignited their collaborative efforts.

With renewed energy, Li Wei and Wu began to experiment with different formulations and applications of the fertilizer, combining Wu's deep understanding of soil properties with Li Wei's expertise in technological applications. They spent long hours in the fields, collecting data, analyzing results, and fine-tuning their approach.

Their perseverance paid off. Slowly but surely, they began to see positive results. The crops treated with their experimental fertilizer showed significant improvement in growth and yield. Encouraged by their success, they expanded their experiments, testing different crops and soil types, and refining their techniques.

Word of their success spread, and soon, other researchers and farmers took notice. Li Wei and Wu's collaborative work became a beacon of innovation, demonstrating the potential of combining traditional agricultural knowledge with modern technological advancements.

Their journey was far from over, but they had laid a strong foundation. Through their partnership, they showed that even the most unlikely collaborations could yield remarkable results when driven by a shared passion and determination. And in the fields of Anhui, amidst the rows of thriving crops, the seeds of their hard work and perseverance began to bear fruit, promising a brighter future for agricultural practices in China and beyond.

田间的火花

为了调研农业应用的可能性，李伟去了不少地方，例如育种、畜牧等。他的旅程充满了好奇心和把先进农业技术带回家乡的愿望。一个偶然的机会，他结识了安徽省农科院的吴文荣，一位长期蹲在农村试验点从事科学施肥研究的土肥专家。

吴文荣是一位在田间耕耘多年的老兵，毕生致力于了解土壤和植物营养的奥秘。相比之下，李伟从美国回来时，只有几篇关于专家系统普适性的资料，对国际农业应用研究一无所知。

从一开始，他们就面临着巨大的挑战。他们没有助手，也没有课题支持。只有他们两个人，来自完全不同的领域，试图交流、分享想法并进行合作。在最初的几个月里，他们的讨论往往毫无结果，难以找到共同点或行动的起点。

随着时间的推移，没有任何实质性进展，他们开始感到沮丧。讨论充满了理论争论和推测性想法，却没有明确的方向或可行的计划。然而，有一天，李伟在翻阅研究报告时，偶然发现了一篇关于砂浆黑土肥料试验的总结报告。在数据和分析的众多页面中，一个特定的肥料效应方程引起了他的注意。

"对呀，就从这里下手!"李伟几乎叫了出来，激动之情溢于言表。

吴文荣走过来，被李伟突如其来的兴奋所吸引。当他们一起深入研究这份报告时，他们意识到这个方程提供了一个可以建立在其上的实际基础。这是一个突破性的时刻，一个点燃他们合作努力的火花。

怀着焕然一新的精力，李伟和吴文荣开始实验不同的肥料配方和应用，结合吴文荣对土壤性质的深刻理解和李伟在技术应用方面的专长。他们在田间度过了漫长的时间，收集数据，分析结果，不断完善他们的方法。

他们的坚持得到了回报。逐渐地，他们开始看到积极的结果。用他们的实验性肥料处理的作物显示出显著的生长和产量改善。在成功的鼓舞下，他们扩大了实验范围，测试不同的作物和土壤类型，并不断优化他们的技术。

他们的成功引起了其他研究人员和农民的注意。李伟和吴文荣的合作工作成为创新的灯塔，展示了结合传统农业知识与现代技术进步的潜力。

他们的旅程远未结束，但他们已经奠定了坚实的基础。通过他们的合作，他们展示了即使是最不可能的合作，只要有共同的激情和决心，也能取得非凡的成果。而在安徽的田间，在茁壮成长的作物行间，他们辛勤工作和坚持不懈的种子开始结果，预示着中国及其他地区农业实践的光明未来。

In fields of amber, where the wind whispers low,
A single spark ignites, a silent afterglow.
No crackling fire, nor blaze of might,
But embers hidden, in the fading light.

A Spark in the Fields, a promise untold,
Of dormant power, waiting to unfold.
Beneath the surface, a restless desire,
To break the stillness, set the world afire.

With patient slumber, the spark takes hold,
Nurtured by secrets, stories yet to be told.
Dry leaves gather, kindling awaits,
A single breath, to change the fates.

The wind picks up, a whisper turns to song,
Fanning the embers, where they don't belong.
A hesitant flicker, then a burst of flame,
Transforming the landscape, whispering its name.

Through crackling stalks, the fire takes flight,
Dancing and swirling, in the fading night.
A primal force, a beauty untamed,
Reshaping the fields, forever rearranged.

But sparks can vanish, as quickly as they rise,
Leaving behind ashes, beneath starlit skies.
A fleeting reminder, of potential's might,
The delicate balance, between darkness and light.

So let us learn from the spark's fleeting show,
To harness its power, where knowledge can grow.
For innovation's flame, though wild and bright,
Can illuminate futures, with wisdom's guiding light.

在琥珀色的田野，风儿低语呢喃，
一个火花点燃，留下无声的余烬。
并非噼啪作响的烈火，亦非强烈的火焰，
而是隐藏在消逝的微光中的余烬。

田野中的火花，一个未曾说出的承诺，
潜伏的力量等待着释放。
表面之下，潜藏着不安分的渴望，
打破寂静，点燃世界。

火花耐心地沉睡，坚定不移，
由秘密和尚未讲述的故事所滋养。
枯叶聚集，引火物等待着，
只需一口呼吸，就能改变命运。

风起时，低语变成歌声，
煽动着不该燃烧的地方的余烬。
犹豫的闪烁，然后火焰爆发，
改变着景观，低语着它的名字。

穿过噼啪作响的茎秆，火苗腾空，
在消逝的夜晚里，跳舞旋转。
一种原始的力量，一种无法驯服的美，
重塑田野，永远改变。

然而火花可以像升起一样迅速消失，
留下灰烬，在星空下。
一个短暂的提醒，潜力之强大，
黑暗与光明之间微妙的平衡。

因此，让我们从火花稍纵即逝的表演中学习，
驾驭它的力量，让知识得以发展。
因为创新的火焰，虽然狂野明亮，
可以用智慧的指引之光照亮未来。

The Fertile Plains: A Story of Innovation and Hope

In the early 1980s, China was on the cusp of transformative change. The government had launched the National Sixth Five-Year Science and Technology Plan, aiming to tackle the country's most pressing issues through scientific advancements. Among the many ambitious projects, one stood out: the comprehensive treatment of the sandy black soil in the Huang-Huai-Hai Plain, a region known for its agricultural potential but plagued by poor soil quality and inadequate farming practices.

Li Wei, a young agronomist with a passion for sustainable farming, found himself drawn to this project. Having grown up in a rural village in Anhui Province, he understood the struggles of farmers all too well. His family had toiled on their small plot of land, barely making ends meet. The idea of using science to improve the lives of millions of farmers resonated deeply with him. Thus, he chose to join the Anhui Agricultural Science Academy, dedicating himself to this crucial research.

The project was daunting. The sandy black soil of the Huang-Huai-Hai Plain, while rich in organic matter, was prone to erosion and nutrient depletion. Traditional farming methods only exacerbated these problems, leading to poor crop yields and economic hardship for the farmers. Li Wei and his team knew that their work could potentially change the fate of this vast agricultural region.

They decided to focus on one of the most critical aspects of farming: wheat fertilization. Wheat was the staple crop in the region, and improving its yield could significantly impact food security and farmers' incomes. Li Wei's approach was meticulous and data-driven. He believed that understanding the soil's unique properties and the specific nutrient needs of wheat would be the key to success.

Months turned into years as the team conducted experiments and field trials. They tested various combinations of fertilizers, soil amendments, and irrigation techniques. Li Wei spent countless hours in the laboratory analyzing soil samples and nutrient levels, while also engaging with local farmers to understand their challenges and gain their trust. He knew that any solution they developed had to be practical and cost-effective for it to be widely adopted.

One crisp autumn morning, Li Wei stood in the middle of a test field, watching as the sun rose over the horizon. The wheat plants swayed gently in the breeze, their golden heads heavy with grain. It was a sight that filled him with hope. The latest trial had shown remarkable results: a significant increase in wheat yield and improved soil health. The combination of slow-release nitrogen fertilizers, organic compost, and precise irrigation scheduling had worked wonders.

Excitedly, Li Wei and his team compiled their findings into a comprehensive report, presenting it to the academy and the local agricultural bureau. The results were met with enthusiasm and approval. The government decided to implement the new fertilization techniques across the Huang-Huai-Hai Plain, providing training and resources to the farmers.

As the new methods were adopted, the transformation was evident. Wheat fields flourished, and the once-struggling farmers saw their hard work bear fruit. Li Wei often visited the villages, seeing firsthand the impact of their research. The smiles of the farmers and the bountiful harvests were the best rewards he could have asked for.

Years later, standing at a podium to receive a national award for his contributions to agriculture, Li Wei reflected on the journey. It had been a challenging and rewarding path, one that had reaffirmed his belief in the power of science to bring about positive change. The sandy black soil of the Huang-Huai-Hai Plain had turned into a symbol of hope and resilience, much like the farmers who tended to it.

And so, Li Wei continued his work, driven by the knowledge that even the smallest grains of sand could be transformed into fertile soil with dedication, innovation, and a deep connection to the land and its people.

肥力的奇迹：创新与希望的故事

上世纪八十年代初，中国正处于变革的边缘。政府启动了国家第六个五年科技计划，旨在通过科学进步解决国家最紧迫的问题。在众多雄心勃勃的项目中，有一个尤为引人瞩目：黄淮海平原砂浆黑土的综合治理，这片地区以其农业潜力闻名，但土壤质量差和农业实践不足是其顽疾。

李伟，一个热衷于可持续农业的年轻农学家，被这个项目吸引。他在安徽省一个农村村庄长大，深知农民的种种困境。他的家人在自家小片土地上辛勤劳作，勉强维持生计。用科学改善数百万农民生活状况的想法深深触动了他。因此，他选择加入安徽农业科学院，致力于这项关键的研究。

这个项目任务艰巨。黄淮海平原的砂浆黑土虽然富含有机物质，却易于侵蚀和养分流失。传统的农业耕作方法更是加剧了这些问题，导致作物产量低下和农民经济困境。李伟和他的团队知道，他们的工作有可能改变这片广阔农业地区的命运。

他们决定集中精力解决农业中最关键的问题之一：小麦施肥。小麦是该地区的主要作物，提高其产量可以显著影响粮食安全和农民的收入。李伟的方法既细致又数据驱动。他相信，了解土壤的独特性质和小麦的具体养分需求将是成功的关键。

数月转眼成年，团队进行了实验和田间试验。他们测试了各种肥料组合、土壤改良剂和灌溉技术。李伟在实验室里花费了无数个小时分析土壤样品和养分水平，同时与当地农民交流，了解他们的困难并赢得他们的信任。他知道，他们开发的任何解决方案都必须实用和经济，以便广泛推广。

一个清晨，李伟站在试验田中央，看着太阳从地平线升起。小麦植株在微风中轻轻摇曳，金黄色的穗子压弯了茎杆。这一景象让他充满了希望。最新的试验显示出了显著的成果：小麦产量显著增加，土壤健康状况得到了改善。慢释放氮肥、有机堆肥和精确的灌溉安排的结合产生了惊人的效果。

激动之余，李伟和他的团队将研究成果编制成全面的报告，提交给科研院所和地方农业局。结果受到了热情和赞许。政府决定在黄淮海平原推广这些新的施肥技术，并为农民提供培训和资源支持。

随着新方法的采纳，转变显而易见。小麦田生机勃勃，曾经挣扎的农民看到了他们辛勤劳动的成果。李伟经常访问这些村庄，亲眼见证研究的影响。农民们的笑容和丰收成为他最好的回报。

多年后，站在领奖台上接受国家农业贡献奖时，李伟回顾了这段旅程。这是一条充满挑战和回报的道路，重新确认了他对科学带来积极改变力量的信念。黄淮海平原的砂浆黑土已经成为希望和韧性的象征，就像那些耕耘土地的农民一样。

因此，李伟继续他的工作，深信即使最微小的沙粒也可以通过奉献、创新和对土地及其人民深刻的连接而变成肥沃的土壤。

The Fertile Plains, a carpet vast,
Where emerald whispers hold the past.
No jeweled crown, nor city grand,
But life unfurls, on fertile land.

Beneath the sun, a golden sea,
Of swaying grain, eternally.
Where roots run deep, and spirits soar,
A symphony of life, forevermore.

The gentle breeze, a lullaby,
As seeds take hold, and dreams don't die.
From humble toil, a harvest grows,
Nourishing all, as knowledge flows.

The farmer's hand, with care it sows,
The seeds of hope, where future glows.
A timeless dance, of earth and sky,
Where generations rise and die.

But fertile plains can hold their scars,

Of battles fought, and fallen stars.
For nature's bounty, hard-won prize,
Can fuel both peace, and war's disguise.

Yet hope remains, a verdant thread,
Woven through fields, where life is bred.
A silent promise, whispered low,
For fertile plains, where futures grow.

So let us walk, with hearts alight,
Across these plains, bathed in sunlight.
For in this land, where stories bloom,
We find our place, dispelling gloom.

肥沃的平原，辽阔的地毯，
翠绿的低语诉说着过往。
并非镶嵌珠宝的王冠，也非宏伟的城市，
而是生命在肥沃的土地上蓬勃发展。

阳光下，金色的海洋，
摇曳的稻谷，永恒存在。
根深蒂固，精神高远，
生命的交响曲，永不停息。

轻柔的微风，犹如催眠曲，
种子生根，梦想永存。
从辛勤的劳作中，收获成长，
滋养万物，知识流动。

农民的手，小心翼翼地播种，
希望的种子，照亮着未来。
大地和天空的永恒舞蹈，
一代又一代兴起消亡。

然而，肥沃的平原也留下了伤痕，
战争的厮杀，陨落的星辰。
大自然的恩赐，来之不易的奖赏，

既能滋养和平，也能成为战争的伪装。

但希望依然存在，一条绿色的线索，
穿过田野，孕育着生命。
一个无声的承诺，轻声低语，
肥沃的平原，未来在这里成长。

让我们怀着明亮的心，向前走，
穿过沐浴阳光的平原。
在这个故事绽放的土地上，
找到我们的位置，驱散黑暗。

Seeds of Innovation

In a prestigious research institute nestled amidst the bustling streets of Beijing, Li Wei, a young scientist with a passion for agricultural technology, stood before his superiors. He presented his proposal on "The Application of Computers in Agriculture" with enthusiasm and conviction, only to be met with immediate dismissal.

"Young man," Director Zhang remarked with a hint of condescension, "such topics are hardly suitable for our institute, let alone national projects. They're too common, too mundane."

Denied official status for his project meant no funding, no dedicated lab space. Yet, Li Wei remained undeterred. Fueled by a strong sense of duty and a deep-seated interest, he rallied his team and embarked on a journey of meticulous planning and technical implementation.

Undeterred by initial setbacks, Li Wei and his team worked tirelessly, navigating through bureaucratic hurdles and skeptical attitudes. They procured used computers and repurposed lab space, turning it into a makeshift workshop for their experiments.

Months turned into years as they refined their algorithms for crop forecasting, developed software for automated irrigation systems, and experimented with drone technology for soil analysis. Their work gained attention from local farmers, who saw firsthand the benefits of these innovations in their yields and efficiency.

However, challenges persisted. Funding remained scarce, and recognition from higher authorities seemed distant. Yet, Li Wei found solace in the incremental successes — the smiles of farmers whose livelihoods improved, the quiet nods of his team as they cracked another technical challenge.

One pivotal day, a visiting delegation from the Ministry of Agriculture witnessed their work in action. They were impressed by the tangible results and the potential for scaling these innovations across rural China. Li Wei's project was finally recognized as a pioneering effort in merging technology with agriculture, earning it the coveted national research status.

As news spread, Li Wei reflected on the journey that began with a simple proposal and faced countless obstacles. It wasn't just about computers in agriculture anymore; it was about resilience, about proving that innovation could sprout from humble beginnings and transform the landscape.

In the end, Li Wei's story echoed through the halls of the institute as a testament to perseverance and the power of an idea that refused to be dismissed.

This story explores themes of innovation, perseverance, and the transformative impact of technology in traditional sectors like agriculture, set against the backdrop of bureaucratic challenges and institutional skepticism.

《创新的种子》

在北京繁华街道间一个声名显赫的研究所里，年轻科学家李伟站在上级面前。他怀着激情和信念提出了关于"计算机在农业中的应用"的建议，却立即遭到了否定。

"年轻人，"张所长带着些许不屑地说道，"这样的课题不适合我们的研究所，更别提国家级项目。太普通，太平凡了。"

因为项目未能获得正式认可，李伟无法获得经费，也无法获得专用实验室空间。然而，李伟并未被打倒。在责任感和浓厚兴趣的驱动下，他率领助手们坚定地投入到了详尽的计划和技术实施之中。

在面对官僚主义障碍和怀疑态度时，李伟和他的团队毫不气馁。他们收集旧电脑，重新利用实验室空间，将其改造成为实验工作室。他们凭借耐心和技术不断优化算法，开发用于自动灌溉系统的软件，并探索用于土壤分析的无人机技术。这些创新工作得到了当地农民的关注，他们亲眼见证了这些技术创新给他们带来的产量提升和效率改进。

然而，挑战仍然存在。资金依然稀缺，来自上级机构的认可似乎遥不可及。尽管如此，李伟在每一次小小的成功中找到了安慰——农民们因他们的生计得到改善而露出的微笑，团队在攻克技术难题时默默点头的肯定。

一天，农业部的代表团突然来访，目睹了他们的工作成果。他们对这些创新的实际效果和在中国农村推广这些创新的潜力印象深刻。李伟的项目终于被认可为将技术与农业结合的开创性工作，获得了令人艳羡的国家级研究地位。

随着消息的传播，李伟回顾起这段旅程，从一个简单的提议开始，面对无数障碍。这不仅仅是关于计算机在农业中的应用，更是关于坚韧不拔，关于证明创新可以从卑微的起点发芽，并改变整个领域的故事。

最终，李伟的故事在研究所的大厅里回响，成为坚持和一个拒绝被否定的想法力量的象征。

In fertile minds, where thoughts take root,
Innovative seeds, a novel fruit.
No farmer's plow, no sunlit soil,
But ideas blossom, breaking the toil.

These innovative seeds, so bright,
Spark solutions, banish night.
They challenge norms, with purpose bold,
Reshaping futures, stories untold.

From labs they spring, with coded might,
To heal the planet, set wrongs to right.
Sustainable whispers, a gentle breeze,
Planting the promise, for future trees.

Biomimicry's touch, a nature's embrace,
Unveiling secrets, at a faster pace.
Materials morph, with wondrous might,
Lighter, stronger, taking flight.

Collaboration's thread, a vibrant weave,
Connecting minds, for problems to cleave.
Sharing knowledge, a boundless sea,
Innovation's tide, forever free.

But with each seed, a choice unfolds,
For progress unchecked, a story untold.
Ethical questions, a cautious tread,
Guiding the future, where hearts are led.

So let us nurture these seeds with care,
With wisdom's hand, and purpose rare.
For innovation's bloom, a powerful thing,
Can heal the world, on hope's soft wing.

在沃腴的思想中，思绪生根发芽，
创新的种子，结出新奇的果实。
并非农夫的犁铧，也非阳光照射的土壤，
而是思想绽放，打破桎梏。

这些创新的种子，如此明亮，
点燃解决方案，驱逐黑暗。
挑战规范，目标坚定而大胆，

重塑未来，讲述未曾言说的故事。

它们从实验室中涌现，蕴含着编码的力量，
治愈星球，纠正错误。
可持续的低语，犹如轻柔的微风，
播种承诺，为未来的树木扎根。

仿生学的触碰，自然的拥抱，
以更快的速度揭开秘密。
材料变形，拥有奇妙的力量，
更轻更强，翱翔天际。

合作的纽带，充满活力的编织，
连接思想，解决难题。
分享知识，浩瀚无边的海洋，
创新的浪潮，永远自由。

但每颗种子都伴随着一个选择，
因为不受控制的进步，意味着未知的故事。
伦理问题，谨慎的步履，
引领未来，跟随心灵的指引。

因此，让我们用心呵护这些种子，
用智慧之手和罕见的决心。
因为创新的绽放，力量强大，
可以在希望的羽翼上，治愈世界。

Harmony of Harvest

In the bustling city of Beijing, amidst the rapid pace of reform and opening-up in 1985, Li Wei stood at the forefront of a quiet revolution. A dedicated soul with a passion for agricultural improvement, Li Wei had tirelessly pursued his vision of integrating artificial intelligence into China's most foundational sector.

For years, burning the midnight oil and persevering against all odds, Li Wei developed the "Sha Jiang Black Soil Wheat Fertilization Computer Expert Consultation System." This innovative system aimed to optimize wheat cultivation in the nutrient-rich but challenging Sha Jiang region. The culmination of his efforts was to be presented at the National Economic Evaluation Conference.

As Li Wei nervously awaited the verdict in the conference hall, renowned Professor Cai, a stalwart in the field of expert systems, took the stage. His eyes scanned the room, and then, with a hint of admiration in his voice, he remarked, "Applying expert systems to agriculture—this was beyond our imagination. But Mr. Li is different. He not only envisioned it but persisted and excelled."

Li Wei's heart swelled with pride as he received accolades from his peers and leaders alike. His system promised to revolutionize agricultural practices across China, bringing efficiency and sustainability to the very heart of the nation's economy. For Li Wei, this success was not just about technological advancement; it was a testament to the belief that diligent effort and innovation could transform even the most traditional sectors.

As the conference concluded and Li Wei stepped out into the Beijing evening, he felt a deep sense of fulfillment. The stars above seemed to shimmer brighter, as if affirming the old adage: "Heaven rewards those with perseverance and determination."

In the months that followed, Li Wei's system was implemented across several agricultural regions, each adopting its principles to suit local conditions. Farmers, once skeptical, now eagerly embraced the new technology, seeing firsthand the benefits it brought to their harvests and livelihoods.

Li Wei's journey was not just a personal triumph but a chapter in China's modernization saga—a story of how one man's vision, fueled by determination and supported by technological innovation, could harmonize tradition with progress, bringing prosperity to the fields and hope to the hearts of countless farmers across the nation.

丰收的和谐

在北京这座喧嚣的城市里，1985 年的改革开放步伐快速进行着，李伟站在一个革新的前沿。他是一个对农业改善充满热情的人，多年来，他不懈地追求将人工智能技术应用于中国最基础的领域。

多年来，李伟不畏艰辛，日夜研发他的"砂姜黑土小麦施肥计算机专家咨询系统"。这个创新系统旨在优化沙江地区富含养分但也充满挑战的小麦种植。他的努力的巅峰将在全国经济评估会议上展示。

当李伟在会议大厅里紧张地等待评审结果时，著名的专家系统学家蔡教授登台发言。他的目光扫视全场，然后，他带着赞赏的口吻说道："将专家系统应用于农业——这超出了我们的想象。但李先生与众不同，他不仅有了想法，而且坚持并取得了卓越的成果。"

李伟因同行和领导的赞誉而心怀自豪。他的系统承诺将彻底改革中国的农业实践，为国家经济的核心带来效率和可持续性。对李伟来说，这个成功不仅仅是技术进步，更是一种坚定不移的努力和创新，能够改变甚至最传统的部门。

随着会议的结束，李伟走出北京的会场，他感到深深的满足。头顶上的星星似乎更加闪耀，仿佛在肯定那句古老的格言："皇天不负有心人。"

随着接下来几个月的实施，李伟的系统在多个农业地区得到应用，每个地方都根据当地的条件采纳了其原则。农民们，曾经怀疑的，现在积极地接受新技术，因为他们亲眼见证了它为他们的收成和生计带来的好处。

李伟的旅程不仅是个人的胜利，更是中国现代化进程中的一章——一个关于一个人愿景的故事，由坚定的努力和技术创新推动，使传统与进步和谐融合，为国家各地的农民带来繁荣和希望。

A symphony of bounty rings,
Where nature's hand and labor sings.
No clashing cymbals, no discordant horn,
But fields of gold, in ripened morn.

Harmony of Harvest, a chorus grand,
Of sun and soil, and human hand.
The farmer's sweat, a vital part,
Nourishing life, with gentle art.

The earth's deep hum, a rhythmic beat,
As roots reach down, for water sweet.
The wind sighs soft, through swaying grain,

A lullaby, for fertile plain.

Machines whir soft, a helping hand,
Gleaning the bounty, across the land.
Technology's touch, a modern score,
Efficiency's whisper, wanting more.

From golden yields, a table spread,
For family, friend, and daily bread.
A shared abundance, hearts content,
Harmony's harvest, heaven-sent.

But harmony's song requires a plea,
For mindful harvest, wild and free.
Respect for creatures, great and small,
Sharing the bounty, for one and all.

So let us raise a grateful voice,
For nature's gifts, and human choice.
May harmony's melody forever ring,
A harvest song, the world to sing.

豐收的和谐奏鸣曲，回荡不息，
自然之手与辛勤劳动共同歌唱。
没有刺耳的铍声，也没有不和谐的号角，
只有金黄的田野，在成熟的早晨。

丰收的和谐，宏伟的合唱，
阳光、土地和人类之手。
农民的汗水，不可或缺的一部分，
用温柔的艺术滋养着生命。

大地深沉的嗡嗡声，一种有节奏的律动，
当根须向下生长，寻找甜蜜的滋养。
微风轻柔地穿过摇曳的麦穗，
摇篮曲，为肥沃的平原而唱。

机器轻轻转动，伸出援手，
在整个土地上收集丰收的礼物。
科技的触碰，现代的乐谱，
效率的低语，渴望更多。

从金黄的收成中，摆满餐桌，
为家人、朋友和日常面包。
丰盛的分享，心满意足，
和谐的收获，天降甘霖。

但和谐的歌曲需要恳求，
为了谨慎的收获，自由自在。
尊重大小生物，
分享丰收，惠及所有人。

让我们扬起感恩的声音，
赞美自然的恩赐和人类的选择。
愿和谐的旋律永远萦绕，
一首丰收的歌曲，传唱世界。

Persistence and Glory

In a remote town, Li Wei was a visionary young scientist deeply passionate about soil science, a field considered unconventional at the time. Many ridiculed him, believing his focus would lead nowhere, dismissing his efforts as a waste of time.

However, Li Wei remained undeterred by external doubts and criticisms. He persevered in his research on soil science, gradually accumulating rich experience and insights. He firmly believed that soil not only formed the foundation of agriculture but also held the key to national prosperity.

Years later, thanks to Li Wei's steadfast dedication, soil science began to gain recognition and respect. His research achievements not only improved soil fertility and crop yields but also played a crucial role in environmental conservation and rural economic development. His team earned acclaim both domestically and internationally, becoming a model of a discipline that benefited the nation and its people.

Meanwhile, another medical expert system overseas gained rapid popularity. They had an early start and abundant resources but lacked deep research and practical application integration. They pursued short-term achievements and fame rather than long-term contributions and lasting impact. Over time, their achievements faded into obscurity, leaving behind a fleeting shadow.

Ultimately, society compared the outcomes of both endeavors, recalling an ancient saying: "Courtesy pays no heed to delays, good food fears no tardiness; true fragrance comes naturally." Li Wei's persistence and dedication not only allowed his career to bloom like a flower but also added a brilliant hue to the progress of the nation and the lives of farmers.

在一个偏远的小城，李伟是一位富有远见的年轻科学家。他热爱土壤学，这在当时被视为不入流的研究领域。许多人嘲笑他，认为他的方向不会有前途，甚至觉得他是在浪费时间。

然而，李伟并没有被外界的质疑和冷眼所动摇。他锲而不舍地投入到土壤学的研究中，通过自己的努力逐渐积累了丰富的经验和见解。他深信，土壤不仅是农业的基础，更是国家繁荣的关键所在。

多年后，随着李伟的坚持和努力，土壤学逐渐被认可并得到重视。他的研究成果不仅帮助改善了农田的肥力和产量，还对环境保护和农村经济起到了重要作用。他的团队在国内外都赢得了声誉，成为了利国利民的学科方向的典范。

与此同时，另一位医学专家系统在国外红红火火地发展起来。他们起步早，资源丰富，但却缺乏深度的研究和实际应用的结合。他们追求的是短期内的成就和名利，而不是长远的贡献和持久的影响力。随着时间的推移，他们的成就逐渐被遗忘，留下了一个匆匆而过的影子。

最终，社会对比两者的结果，不禁想起一句古语："有礼不怕迟，好饭不怕晚，是花自然香。"李伟的坚持与执着，不仅让他的事业如花般绽放，也为国家的进步和农民的生活增添了一抹璀璨的色彩。

With steady steps, on path unknown,
Persistence whispers, "Carry on."
No grand fanfare, no trumpet's call,
But a quiet strength, that conquers all.

Through trials faced, and mountains high,
A burning ember in the eye.
The will to rise, though shadows creep,
In every hurdle, a promise to keep.

For glory's light, at journey's end,
Is not a crown, for which to contend.
But the inner peace, a hard-won prize,
The victor's smile, in weary eyes.

The failures faced, the lessons learned,
Each scar a map, where courage burned.
The path unfolds, a winding maze,
Persistence guiding through the daze.

For glory's not a fleeting chime,
But the echo of effort, that stands the test of time.
It's knowing deep within your soul,
You reached the peak, and made yourself whole.

So let us walk, with purpose bold,
Embrace the struggle, let the story unfold.
For in persistence, glory lies,
A tapestry woven, beneath hopeful skies.

坚定步伐，踏上未知之路，
坚持低语，"继续前进吧。"
没有隆重的欢呼，没有喇叭的召唤，
只有默默的力量，征服一切。

面对考验，翻越高山，
眼中燃烧着炽热的火苗。
意志要崛起，即使阴影蔓延，
每个障碍，都是一个承诺的坚守。

因为旅途的终点，荣耀的光芒，
并非争夺的王冠。
而是内心的平和，来之不易的奖赏，
胜利者的微笑，在疲惫的双眼里。

面对的失败，学到的教训，
每一道疤痕，都是勇气燃烧的地图。
道路蜿蜒曲折，不断延伸，
坚持不懈地指引着走出迷茫。

荣耀不是转瞬即逝的钟声，
而是经得起时间考验的努力的回响。
内心深处知晓着，
你登上了顶峰，让自我变得完整。

让我们带着坚定的目标前进，
迎接挑战，让故事展开。
因为坚持之中蕴含着荣耀，
一幅织锦，编织在充满希望的天空下。

The Triumph of Perseverance Li Wei's Journey to Revolutionize Agriculture

In the heart of rural China, amidst the golden fields of wheat and the scent of freshly turned soil, Li Wei embarked on a quest that would redefine the future of farming. His vision, the "Sand Ginger Black Soil Wheat Fertilization Expert Consultation System," aimed to revolutionize agricultural practices through advanced technology.

Li Wei, a seasoned computer scientist with a passion for agriculture, assembled a dedicated team to develop China's first agricultural expert system. The journey was fraught with challenges from the outset. Choosing Basic language for artificial intelligence programming was met with skepticism, deemed by many as impractical for such a sophisticated task. Undeterred, Li Wei led his team down what seemed like an improbable path.

Their first hurdle was gaining acceptance and funding. In a landscape dominated by traditional farming methods, convincing stakeholders of the potential of AI in agriculture was no easy feat. Li Wei tirelessly advocated for his project, citing the efficiency gains and sustainability benefits it could bring to China's agricultural sector.

As months turned into years, the team faced technical setbacks and resource constraints. Basic language, though unconventional, proved to be a double-edged sword—simple yet challenging to scale for complex agricultural algorithms. Despite setbacks, Li Wei's unwavering determination and his team's resilience forged a bond that strengthened with every obstacle overcome.

Their breakthrough came when they successfully integrated Basic with machine learning algorithms tailored for soil analysis and wheat fertilization. The system began to demonstrate its potential, accurately predicting optimal fertilization schedules and soil health improvements. Farmers who initially doubted the system's capabilities were now witnessing firsthand its transformative impact on crop yields and sustainability.

The journey of creating the "Sand Ginger Black Soil Wheat Fertilization Expert Consultation System" became a symbol of innovation in China's agricultural landscape. Li Wei and his team's dedication not only validated the use of AI in farming but also set a precedent for future technological advancements in rural development.

Today, Li Wei's system is celebrated as a pioneering achievement, recognized nationally for its role in modernizing agricultural practices and promoting sustainable farming methods across China. His story serves as a testament to the power of perseverance and innovation in overcoming adversity to achieve groundbreaking success.

攻坚克难的胜利：李伟改革农业之路

在中国农村的心脏地带，金黄色的麦田和新翻的泥土气息中，李伟开始了一场将重新定义农业未来的探索。他的愿景，"砂姜黑土小麦施肥计算机专家咨询系统"，旨在通过先进技术彻底改革农业实践。

李伟是一位经验丰富的计算机科学家，对农业充满热情，他组建了一个专注的团队来开发中国第一个农业专家系统。这段旅程从一开始就充满了挑战。选择 Basic 语言进行人工智能编程引起了人们的怀疑，许多人认为这对于如此复杂的任务来说是不切实际的。然而，李伟毫不气馁，带领团队走上了一条看似不可能的道路。

他们首先面临的障碍是获得认可和资金支持。在传统农业方法主导的背景下，说服利益相关者相信人工智能在农业中的潜力并不容易。李伟不知疲倦地为他的项目辩护，引用其能够为中国农业部门带来的效率提升和可持续发展的好处。

随着时间的推移，团队面临技术挫折和资源限制。Basic 语言虽然不寻常，但却是一把双刃剑，简单而具有挑战性，对复杂的农业算法进行扩展。尽管遇到挫折，李伟坚定不移的决心和团队的韧性在每一次克服困难中加强了团队的凝聚力。

他们的突破发生在成功地将 Basic 语言与专门用于土壤分析和小麦施肥的机器学习算法集成时。系统开始展示其潜力，准确预测最佳施肥计划和土壤健康改善。最初怀疑系统能力的农民们现在亲眼见证了其在提高作物产量和促进可持续发展方面的革命性影响。

创建"砂姜黑土小麦施肥计算机专家咨询系统"的旅程成为了中国农业领域创新的象征。李伟及其团队的奉献精神不仅验证了人工智能在农业中的应用，而且为未来农村发展中的技术进步树立了榜样。

今天，李伟的系统被誉为开创性的成就，在全国范围内因其在现代化农业实践和推广可持续农业方法中的作用而受到赞扬。他的故事是坚持和创新的力量的明证，克服困难并取得开创性成功的故事。

In fields of doubt, where shadows lie,
A single seed, it dares to try.
No fertile ground, no gentle rain,
But hope's lone spark, to ease the pain.

The Triumph of Perseverance, a tale untold,
Of struggles faced, and battles bold.
With roots that dig, through barren earth,
A silent strength, defying birth.

The scorching sun, a relentless heat,

The biting wind, a winter's feat.
But still it climbs, with purpose true,
Reaching for sunlight, breaking through.

Through cracks it crawls, a fragile shoot,
Defying odds, with resolute loot.
A single leaf, unfurled so bright,
A testament to endless fight.

The doubts may whisper, voices low,
"This dream's too big, let it go."
But perseverance's fire burns strong,
A steady beat, a victory song.

For in the triumph, there's no fanfare,
Just quiet bloom, beneath the stare.
A vibrant flower, reaching high,
A silent shout, against the sky.

So let us learn, from this small seed,
The power of will, the planted creed.
For even in darkness, life can start,
With perseverance, playing its part.

在怀疑的田野里，阴影笼罩，
一颗种子，它敢于尝试。
没有肥沃的土地，没有温柔的雨水，
只有希望的孤星，减轻痛苦。

坚持的胜利，一个未曾讲述的故事，
面对的斗争，和勇敢的战斗。
根茎扎入贫瘠的土地，
一种无声的力量，蔑视着诞生。

烈日炎炎，无情的酷暑，
刺骨的寒风，冬天的壮举。
但它仍以坚定不移的信念攀爬，
追逐阳光，突破束缚。

穿过裂缝，它是一个脆弱的嫩芽，
无视困难，以坚定的战利品对抗。
一片叶子，明亮地舒展开来，
为永无止境的战斗作证。

怀疑的声音可能低声耳语，
"这个梦想太大，放弃吧。"
但坚持不懈的火焰燃烧得更旺盛，
一个稳定的节拍，胜利的歌曲。

因为在胜利中，没有欢呼喝彩，
只有静静绽放的花朵，在凝视之下。
一朵鲜艳的花朵，高高地伸展着，
对天空中无声的呐喊。

所以让我们从这颗小小的种子中学习，
意志的力量，种下的信条。
因为即使在黑暗中，生活也可以开始，
坚持不懈地发挥着它的作用。

Knowledge is power

In a bustling research laboratory nestled within the heart of Beijing, Li Wei and his team of experts were deeply immersed in their quest to advance the field of expert systems—a cornerstone of artificial intelligence. At that time, the prevailing international standard was the rule-based representation method, where each unit of knowledge was dissected into independent rules. This approach was ideal for straightforward logical knowledge but fell short when dealing with the complex interplay of empirical and computational knowledge, such as analyzing fertilization techniques.

Li Wei, renowned for his innovative spirit, recognized the limitations of the existing methods. He and his team embarked on a journey of experimentation and discovery, driven by a singular goal: to create a synthesis that could seamlessly integrate both deductive and computational rules, thereby revolutionizing the approach to knowledge representation in expert systems.

Days turned into weeks as the team meticulously tested and refined their hybrid approach. They faced numerous challenges and setbacks, but their unwavering determination fueled their progress. Slowly but steadily, patterns began to emerge from the sea of data they had amassed. Insights gleaned from practical farming experiences were interwoven with the precision of computational algorithms, forming a cohesive framework that surpassed their initial expectations.

The breakthrough came during a late-night session, where Li Wei, surrounded by equations and diagrams, had a moment of clarity. He scribbled furiously on his notepad, outlining the unified rule set that bridged the gap between logic-driven reasoning and data-driven computation. It was a eureka moment—the birth of a new paradigm in knowledge representation.

Armed with their revolutionary approach, Li Wei's team presented their findings at an international conference on artificial intelligence. Initially met with skepticism, their presentation gradually captivated the audience as they demonstrated the effectiveness of their synthesized rule group representation. Experts from around the world marveled at the elegance and practicality of their solution, heralding it as a significant leap forward in the field.

As accolades poured in and invitations for collaborations flooded their inboxes, Li Wei reflected on the journey that led them here. It wasn't just about innovation; it was about pushing boundaries and redefining what was possible in the realm of artificial intelligence. Their success underscored the power of perseverance and interdisciplinary collaboration—a testament to the transformative potential of merging logical and computational knowledge.

In the annals of AI history, Li Wei's synthesis of knowledge remains a shining example of how innovation thrives at the intersection of theory and practice—a beacon of inspiration for future generations of researchers and pioneers in the field of artificial intelligence.

知识就是力量

在北京繁华的研究实验室中，李伟和他的专家团队全神贯注地致力于推进专家系统领域——这是人工智能的核心技术之一。当时，国际上通行的是基于规则的知识表示方法，即将每个知识单元分解为独立的规则。这种方法适合简单的逻辑知识，但在处理施肥技术等复杂的经验与计算知识交互的场景下显得力不从心。

以创新精神著称的李伟意识到现有方法的局限性。他和他的团队展开了一段实验与探索之旅，目标是创造一种能够无缝整合演绎与计算规则的综合方法，从而彻底改变专家系统中的知识表示方法。

日复一日，他们不断地进行试验和完善。团队面临诸多挑战和挫折，但他们坚定的决心驱使着他们前行。渐渐地，他们从积累的海量数据中发现了规律。从实际农业经验中得到的见解与精确的计算算法相结合，形成了一个连贯的框架，远远超出了他们最初的预期。

突破发生在一个深夜的研讨会上。李伟被方程式和图表包围，突然间他有了灵感。他在记事本上狂笔乱画，勾勒出了能够弥合逻辑推理和数据计算之间鸿沟的统一规则集。这是一个顿悟的时刻——知识表示领域的新范式诞生了。

凭借他们的革新方法，李伟的团队在国际人工智能会议上展示了他们的发现。起初遭遇怀疑，但随着他们展示出综合规则组表示方法的有效性，观众逐渐被他们的演示所吸引。来自世界各地的专家们惊叹于他们解决方案的优雅和实用性，将其视为该领域的重大进步。

随着荣誉的涌现和合作邀请的蜂拥而至，李伟回顾了他们走过的道路。这不仅仅是关于创新，更是关于突破界限、重新定义人工智能领域可能性的旅程。他们的成功彰显了毅力和跨学科合作的力量——这是将理论与实践融合的转型潜力的明证。

在人工智能历史的编年史中，李伟的知识综合方法仍然是一个光辉的例子，展示了创新在理论与实践交汇处的力量——对未来研究者和人工智能领域先驱的启示。

In simplicity's embrace, a strength untold,
Where essence lies, pure and bold.
"Just is just," a mantra true,
A beacon bright, guiding you.

In nature's art, a symphony grand,
Where elements blend, hand in hand.
The flowing stream, the soaring sky,
In their "just is," their beauty lies.

The humble flower, petals unfurled,
In its "just is," a radiant world.

The gentle breeze, whispering through trees,
In its "just is," a symphony of ease.

In human touch, a warmth so deep,
Where hearts connect, in slumbered sleep.
The tender smile, the kind embrace,
In their "just is," love finds its place.

In words unspoken, emotions clear,
In "just is," understanding near.
A silent glance, a knowing gaze,
In their "just is," truth softly plays.

In quiet moments, thoughts serene,
Where minds unwind, thoughts convene.
The gentle breath, the steady beat,
In their "just is," peace finds its seat.

So let us seek, in life's grand quest,
The power of "just," put to the test.
In simplicity's embrace, let's find our way,
Where "just is just," and strength holds sway.

简朴的拥抱中，蕴藏着无言的力量，
本质所在，纯净而张扬。
"只是就是"，真言至理，
指引你的明亮灯塔。

自然之美，宏伟交响，
元素交融，携手并肩。
流淌的溪流，高耸的天空，
"只是如此"，便成就了美丽。

朴素的花朵，花瓣舒展，
"只是如此"，便是光明的世界。
温柔的微风，穿过树林低语，
"只是如此"，便是轻松的交响曲。

人类的触碰，温暖深切，
心与心相连，沉睡入梦。
温柔的微笑，友善的拥抱，
"只是如此"，爱便找到了归宿。

在无声的话语中，情感清晰，
"只是如此"，理解就在咫尺。
一个无声的眼神，一个理解的目光，
"只是如此"，真理悄然展现。

在静谧的时刻，思绪宁静，
心灵放松，思绪聚集。
轻柔的呼吸，稳定的心跳，
"只是如此"，平静便找到了安息之处。

因此，让我们在人生的伟大追求中，
寻求"只是"的力量，接受考验。
在朴实的拥抱中找到我们的道路，
"只是就是"，让力量主宰。

Language is the BASIC

In a quiet corner of the Hefei Botanical Garden, Li Wei hurried past, his heart full of anticipation for the upcoming national artificial intelligence academic conference. As a pioneer in the field of AI, he was accustomed to collisions and challenges with traditional thinking. This conference, he planned to share his latest research on expert systems, an innovative approach based on Basic language.

At the conference, Li Wei's technological approach sparked controversy. Some questioned why he didn't use advanced AI languages like Lisp or Prolog, believing only these could truly be called intelligent systems. Yet Li Wei never wavered, firm in his belief that the value of technology lay in practicality and efficiency rather than complexity and trendiness.

Years later, facts proved his persistence right. In the early 1990s, the international community began to reconsider the limitations of traditional AI languages, with more and more systems adopting simpler, more efficient programming languages, even assembly language. These changes mirrored the path Li Wei had tried and implemented in the early 1980s.

On a spring afternoon in the Hefei Botanical Garden, Li Wei stood under the azure sky, reflecting on his research journey. His expert systems now played a crucial role in various fields, not only validating his technological choices but also becoming part of the history of AI development. He knew deep down that practice brings true knowledge. Despite any doubts or opposition he faced, as long as he remained steadfast in his beliefs and direction, he would eventually shine in his own moment of glory.

语言是最基本的

在合肥植物园的一座宁静角落，李伟匆匆走过，心中满是对即将到来的全国人工智能学术会议的期待。作为人工智能领域的先驱，他早已习惯了与传统思维的碰撞和挑战。这次会议，他准备分享他最新的专家系统研究成果，一种以 Basic 语言为基础的创新方法。

会议上，李伟的技术路线引起了不少争议。一些人质疑他为何不使用像 Lisp、Prolog 这样的高级人工智能语言，认为只有这样才能真正称得上智能系统。然而，李伟从不为此动摇，因为他深信，技术的价值在于实用性和效率，而非复杂度和流行。

多年后的事实证明了他的坚持。九十年代初期，国际上开始反思使用传统人工智能语言的局限性，越来越多的系统开始采用更简单、更高效的编程语言，甚至是汇编语言。这些变革，正是李伟早在八十年代初期就已经尝试和实施的路径。

在合肥植物园的那个春日午后，李伟站在蔚蓝天空下，回顾自己的科研之路。他的专家系统，如今在各个领域发挥着重要作用，不仅证明了他的技术选择的正确性，更成为了人工智能发展史上的一部分。他深知，实践出真知，无论遇到多少质疑和反对，只要坚持自己的信念和方向，最终都会迎来属于自己的那一刻光芒。

In realms of silicon, where circuits weave,
A language of logic, ASICs conceive.
With gates and cells, a symphony grand,
They shape the world, with an iron hand.

In tiny transistors, a world unfolds,
Where bits and bytes, in stories are told.
ASICs, the architects, of digital dreams,
Designing circuits, where data gleams.

From smartphones sleek, to computers grand,
ASICs empower, with an unseen hand.
They process signals, with lightning speed,
Enabling wonders, that we can't impede.

In medical devices, life's fragile thread,
ASICs safeguard, with watchful tread.
Monitoring rhythms, with precision keen,
Ensuring well-being, a vital scene.

In vehicles that roam, both land and air,
ASICs control, with utmost care.
Optimizing engines, with fuel-efficient grace,
Ensuring journeys, with safety's embrace.

In homes we dwell, where comforts reside,
ASICs connect, with circuits as guides.
Regulating systems, with a watchful eye,
Ensuring warmth and light, beneath the sky.

Oh, ASICs, marvels of human art,
Your language of logic, plays a vital part.
Shaping our world, with silent might,
A symphony of silicon, shining bright.

So let us honor, these tiny gems,

ASICs, the language, that technology stems.
Their power and brilliance, a testament to our skill,
In shaping the future, with unwavering will.

在硅的世界里，电路交织，
ASIC 构思着逻辑的语言。
以门和单元，奏出宏伟的交响乐，
它们塑造着世界，铁腕掌控。

在微小的晶体管中，一个世界展开，
比特和字节，在故事中诉说。
ASIC，数字梦想的建筑师，
设计电路，让数据闪耀。

从时尚的智能手机到宏伟的电脑，
ASIC 赋予力量，无形之手。
它们以闪电般的速度处理信号，
实现奇迹，势不可挡。

在医疗设备中，生命脆弱的线头，
ASIC 守护着，步履谨慎。
以敏锐的精度监测着节律，
确保福祉，至关重要的场景。

在陆地和空中的交通工具中，
ASIC 控制着，细致入微。
以节能优雅优化引擎，
确保旅程，安全呵护。

在我们居住的房屋里，舒适安居，
ASIC 连接着，电路作为指引。
用警惕的眼睛监管系统，
确保天空下的温暖和光明。

哦，**ASIC**，人类艺术的奇迹，

你的逻辑语言，扮演着至关重要的角色。
用无声的力量塑造着我们的世界，
硅的交响曲，闪耀着光芒。

因此，让我们赞颂这些微小的宝石，
ASIC，技术源泉的语言。
它们的力量和智慧，是我们技能的证明，
以坚定不移的意志塑造未来。

The Knowledge Harvesters

In a quiet corner of a bustling city, nestled among rows of nondescript office buildings, Li Wei and his team embarked on a journey into the unknown world of agricultural technology. Armed with determination and a pioneering spirit, they faced the daunting task of creating a knowledge repository crucial for their ambitious expert system.

Li Wei, a software engineer by training, found himself thrust into unfamiliar territory the moment the project's technical roadmap was set. Collaborating with domain experts to compile this repository became the linchpin of their endeavor. However, neither Li Wei nor his team had ever tackled such a meticulous and complex task before. To complicate matters further, they possessed zero expertise in agricultural technology—a critical factor in determining the success of their expert system.

Undeterred by the enormity of the challenge, Li Wei's team approached the task with the philosophy of "eating the crab first" and the resolve to "gnaw through bones like ants." They embarked on a painstaking journey of exploration and experimentation, one step at a time.

Li Wei's mind was both agile and meticulous. Once the primary functions were defined, he delved into the intricate thought processes of agricultural experts, particularly their nuanced analysis of scientific fertilization. Questions like how to determine fertility levels based on soil's physical and chemical parameters—organic matter, available nitrogen, phosphorus, potassium, total nitrogen, phosphorus, pH levels, bulk density, porosity, plow layer thickness, irrigation and drainage conditions—loomed large before them.

Every day was a blend of frustration and breakthroughs. They wrestled with data, often spending hours deciphering technical papers and consulting with reluctant experts who were initially skeptical of their software-driven approach.

As weeks turned into months, Li Wei and his team began to make headway. They crafted algorithms that mimicked the decision-making processes of seasoned agronomists, creating a virtual brain that could reason and recommend based on vast pools of agricultural wisdom.

Their breakthrough moment came during a late-night session when Li Wei cracked a particularly stubborn problem related to soil pH variability. It was a eureka moment that reverberated through their small office, marking a turning point in their journey towards creating a functional, reliable expert system.

Months of tireless effort culminated in a prototype that impressed even the most skeptical of experts. The knowledge repository they painstakingly compiled became the backbone of their system, a testament to their perseverance and willingness to venture into uncharted waters.

As they presented their work to stakeholders and potential users, Li Wei couldn't help but reflect on the journey. What started as a technical challenge evolved into a testament to human determination and the power of collaborative innovation. In the end, their project not only promised to revolutionize agricultural technology but also stood as a testament to the limitless possibilities when courage and diligence converge.

In the annals of their company's history, this project would be remembered as the moment when a team of software engineers dared to harvest knowledge from the fields of experts, turning uncertainty into a beacon of progress.

知识的收割者们

在繁华城市的一角，一群人在一排普通的办公楼中开启了一段关于农业技术的未知之旅。李伟和他的团队凭借着决心和开拓精神，迎接着一个艰巨的任务——创建一个对于他们雄心勃勃的专家系统至关重要的知识库。

李伟，一个以软件工程为背景的工程师，在项目的技术路线确定后，立即发现自己被推到了一个陌生的领域。与领域专家合作编制知识库成为了他们工作的关键所在。然而，李伟及其团队在这方面完全没有经验，这让任务变得更加艰巨。特别是他们对农业技术一窍不通，而这正是决定他们的专家系统能否成功的关键因素之一。

尽管面对巨大的挑战，李伟和他的团队并没有退缩。他们以"先吃螃蟹"的勇气和"蚂蚁啃骨头"的决心，一步步地探索和试验。

李伟的思维跳跃而细腻。一旦确定了主要功能，他便深入研究农业专家们复杂而微妙的思维过程，尤其是他们在科学施肥方面的细致分析。他们面对的问题包括如何根据土壤的物理和化学参数确定肥力水平——如有机物质含量、速效氮、速效磷、速效钾、总氮、总磷、PH 值、容重、孔隙度、耕层厚度、排灌条件等。

每一天都是挑战和突破的交织。他们不断地与数据搏斗，常常花费数小时来解读技术论文，并与起初对他们采用软件驱动方法持怀疑态度的专家们进行咨询。

随着时间的推移，李伟和他的团队开始取得进展。他们开发出模仿资深农学家决策过程的算法，创造了一个能够基于广泛的农业智慧进行推理和建议的虚拟大脑。

他们的突破时刻是在一个深夜的工作中到来的，当李伟解决了一个关于土壤 PH 值变异的棘手问题时。这是一个令人振奋的时刻，它标志着他们在创造一个功能齐备、可靠的专家系统的旅程中迈出了重要一步。

数月的不懈努力最终促成了一个原型，即使是最为怀疑的专家们也被他们的成果所打动。他们辛苦编制的知识库成为了他们系统的核心，它是他们毅力和愿意冒险探索未知的证明。

当他们向利益相关者和潜在用户展示他们的工作时，李伟不禁反思起这段旅程。这个项目从一个技术挑战演变成了人类决心和协作创新的典范。最终，他们的项目不仅承诺革新农业技术，也成为勇气和勤奋汇聚时无限可能的象征。

在公司历史的长河中，这个项目将被铭记为一个软件工程团队敢于从专家的领域中收割知识，将不确定性转化为进步的时刻。

In fields of thought, where wisdom grows,
The Knowledge Harvesters, their spirit glows.
No farmer's scythe, nor sun-kissed grain,
But minds that glean, to ease life's pain.

With tireless hands, they sift and sort,
The facts and truths, in wisdom's court.
From dusty tomes, to screens alight,
They gather knowledge, burning bright.

They delve in depths, where secrets hide,
Unraveling mysteries, with minds as guide.
Through history's weave, and science' quest,
They glean the harvest, put it to the test.

With curious hearts, and questions bold,
They challenge norms, the stories told.
For knowledge thrives, in open ground,
Where doubt is welcomed, a fertile sound.

They bridge the gaps, with open hand,
Connecting minds, across the land.
Sharing their bounty, a flowing stream,
Inspiring others, to chase life's dream.

But knowledge, like a seed, must grow,
Nurtured with care, to help it flow.
Planted in action, for all to see,
A harvest shared, for humanity.

So let us raise a voice of praise,
For Knowledge Harvesters, in wisdom's maze.
For in their gleaning, a future gleams,
A world enlightened, by their noble dreams.

在思想的田野里，智慧生长，
知识收割者，精神闪耀。
没有农夫的镰刀，也无阳光照耀的谷粒，
只有勤奋的头脑，为减轻生活痛苦而精心筛选。

他们用不知疲倦的双手筛选和分类，
智慧法庭里的事实和真理。
从蒙尘的古籍到亮丽的屏幕，
他们聚集知识，熊熊燃烧。

他们深入探索隐藏的深处，揭开秘密，
以思想为指引，解开谜团。
穿越历史的织锦和科学的探索，
他们收集收获，加以检验。

他们怀着好奇的心和大胆的问题，
挑战规范，讲述的故事。
因为知识在开放的土地上茁壮成长，
质疑在这里被欢迎，这是肥沃的土壤。

他们张开双手搭建桥梁，
连接思想，跨越疆域。
分享他们的慷慨，涓涓细流，
激励他人，追逐人生梦想。

但知识就像种子，必须生长，
精心培育，才能让它流动。
种植在行动中，供所有人看到，
共享的收获，为人道主义。

让我们为知识收割者喝彩，
在智慧的迷宫中。
因为在他们的收获中，未来闪耀着光芒，
一个被他们崇高梦想照亮的的世界。

The Soil Whisperer

In the heart of rural China, where the land stretches out under vast skies, Li Wei pursued his passion for agricultural science with relentless dedication. His days were consumed by the intricacies of soil fertility, a subject that seemed to weave its mysteries into the very fabric of his being.

It was a brisk morning when Li Wei found himself deep in conversation with a local farmer, Mr. Zhang, whose fields had been struggling with declining yields. "But how do we determine soil fertility when not all farmers have complete soil parameters?" Mr. Zhang asked, a furrow forming on his weathered brow.

Li Wei nodded thoughtfully, knowing well the disparities that plagued rural farming communities. "We rely on the main soil parameters we can gather," he explained patiently. "But these parameters often vary. Some farmers might not have any soil data at all."

Mr. Zhang sighed, his gaze fixed on the distant fields where green shoots struggled to thrive. "And if there's no data, how do we know how much fertilizer to use?"

Li Wei smiled reassuringly. "Sometimes, we look to the past. We assess the yields of the last three years to estimate soil fertility," he suggested. "And we consider using locally trusted methods, like applying farmyard manure."

This sparked a glimmer of hope in Mr. Zhang's eyes. "But different soil fertilities require different amounts of nitrogen, phosphorus, and potassium," he interjected, eager to understand the nuances.

"Exactly," Li Wei replied, his voice gentle yet resolute. "The amount and timing of fertilizers—both basal and top dressing—vary with soil fertility levels. We also factor in planting seasons and adjust chemical fertilizer quantities based on organic inputs."

Months passed, marked by Li Wei's tireless research and meticulous trials in Mr. Zhang's fields. With each visit, he fine-tuned his calculations and recommendations, blending scientific rigor with local wisdom.

Then, one autumn afternoon, under the golden hues of a setting sun, Li Wei presented Mr. Zhang with the results. "Your soil, Mr. Zhang, thrives on a balanced mix of nutrients," he announced, holding out a detailed fertilization plan. "This should improve your yields significantly next season."

Mr. Zhang clasped the paper with reverence, his gratitude palpable. "You've brought us hope, Mr. Li," he said warmly. "Your patient determination and scientific spirit have given birth to something truly remarkable."

Li Wei smiled modestly, knowing that behind every successful formula lay countless hours of meticulous effort and unwavering belief in the power of science to transform lives.

And thus, in the quiet corners of rural China, where the earth whispered its secrets to those who listened, Li Wei's legacy grew—a testament to the profound impact of dedication, innovation, and a deep respect for the land.

This story celebrates the dedication of scientists like Li Wei who work tirelessly to improve agricultural practices and uplift rural communities through their expertise and empathy.

土壤的耳语者

在中国农村广袤的天空下，李伟全心投入于农业科学的研究之中，他对土壤肥力的探索充满了坚定的热情。他的日子被那些错综复杂的土壤肥力问题所充斥，仿佛这些问题已经融入到他的生活中。

一个清晨，李伟与当地农民张老板深入交谈，张老板的田地产量一直在下降，他忧心忡忡地问道："但如果农户没有完整的土壤参数，我们怎么确定土壤的肥力呢？"他的额头布满了岁月的痕迹。

李伟深思地点点头，深知困扰农村农民社区的差异。"我们依赖于我们能够收集到的主要土壤参数，"他耐心地解释道，"但这些参数经常会有所不同。有些农民甚至可能根本没有任何土壤数据。"

张老板叹了口气，目光投向远方那些艰难生长的绿色嫩苗。"如果没有数据，我们如何知道要施用多少肥料呢？"他焦急地问道。

李伟微笑着安慰道："有时候，我们可以回顾过去。我们评估过去三年的产量来估算土壤的肥力，"他建议道，"同时，我们考虑采用当地信任的方法，比如施用农家肥。"

这一建议让张老板眼中闪现出一丝希望。"但不同的土壤肥力需要不同数量的氮、磷、钾肥料，"他插话道，渴望理解这些微妙的差异。

"确实如此，"李伟声音温和而坚定，"基肥和追肥的量和时机取决于土壤肥力水平。我们还会考虑播种季节，并根据有机肥的使用量调整化肥的施用。"

几个月过去了，在李伟在张老板田地里不懈的研究和细致的试验中。每次访问，他都在精心调整他的计算和建议，将科学严谨与当地智慧融合在一起。

然后，一个秋日的下午，在金色的夕阳中，李伟向张老板展示了他的研究成果。"张老板，你的土壤需要一种均衡的营养混合物，"他宣布道，递上了一份详细的施肥计划，"这应该会显著提高下一个季节的产量。"

张老板敬畏地接过纸张，"你给我们带来了希望，李先生，"他温暖地说道，"你不厌其烦的研究精神和科学态度，创造了一些真正卓越的成果。"

李伟谦逊地微笑着，他知道每一个成功的配方背后都有无数个小时的精心工作和对科学改变生活的坚定信念。

于是，在中国农村的静谧角落里，那些倾听大地秘密的人，李伟的遗产在慢慢成形——这是对奉献、创新以及对土地深深敬畏的生动诠释。

这个故事赞颂了像李伟这样的科学家，他们不懈地努力改善农业实践，通过他们的专业知识和对土地的尊重，提升了农村社区的生活质量。

The Soil whispers, a voice unseen,
A chorus ancient, evergreen.
No human tongue, no trumpet's blare,
But secrets kept, with subtle care.

It speaks of life, in cycles grand,
From fallen seed, to reaching hand.
The patient hum of slow decay,
That nourishes life, day by day.

It whispers tales of sun and rain,
Of roots that delve, through earth's domain.
Of silent battles, fought unseen,
Where life persists, in verdant green.

It murmurs warnings, soft and low,
Of human greed, and careless flow.
The scars of waste, the land laid bare,
A silent plea, for mindful care.

But hope remains, a fertile thread,
Woven through whispers, gently said.
Of resilience strong, and life's embrace,
The Soil whispers, for a better space.

So let us listen, with hearts attuned,
To the wisdom whispered, from the ground.
For in its voice, a truth unfolds,
A story waiting, to be told.

With gentle touch, and purpose true,
We'll nurture life, where whispers flow anew.
For the Soil's soft song, a sacred trust,
A promise whispered, from the dust.

泥土低语，无声的诉说，
古老的合唱，长青不衰。
并非人类的语言，也非喇叭的喧嚣，
而是细心守护的秘密，低语浅道。

它讲述着生命周而复始的宏大循环，
从落下的种子，到伸出的援手。
耐心低吟着缓慢腐烂的旋律，
日复一日，滋养着生命。

它低语着阳光和雨水的传说，
根须深入大地深处，探索着领地。
无声的战斗，肉眼难辨，
生命顽强地坚持着，一片翠绿。

它轻声细语地发出警告，柔和而低沉，
关于人类的贪婪和肆意挥霍。
浪费的伤疤，裸露的土地，
一个无声的请求，呼吁人们细心呵护。

但希望依然存在，一根肥沃的线，

编织在轻柔的低语中。
强大的韧性和生命的拥抱，
泥土低语，期盼更美好的空间。

让我们用心聆听，与大地协调，
来自地下的低语声中蕴含的智慧。
因为它的声音中，一个真理正在展开，
一个等待讲述的故事。

以轻柔的触碰和真诚的意图，
我们将呵护生命，让低语再次流淌。
泥土的轻柔歌声，神圣的信任，
来自尘埃的低语，一个承诺。

AI Field Fertilization

In a quiet village nestled among the golden wheat fields of northern China, a technological revolution quietly unfolded. Li Wei, a computer expert specializing in agricultural systems, unveiled his latest creation: the "Sand Ginger Black Soil Wheat Fertilization Expert Consultation System." This innovation promised to transform farming practices by optimizing fertilizer application for wheat crops, aiming to increase yields while reducing waste.

Excited murmurs spread through the agricultural community as Li Wei's system underwent rigorous field trials. The initial results were astonishingly accurate, with deviations in yield estimations averaging just 3.26% for over-fertilized scenarios and a mere 2.65% for optimally fertilized fields. These findings exposed prevalent inefficiencies in local farming practices.

In the field trials, it became evident that some farmers were applying excessive nitrogen, neglecting phosphorus entirely, leading to wheat lodging and significant yield losses. Not only did this misuse of fertilizers waste resources, but it also diminished crop yields by several hundred pounds per acre. Conversely, other farmers, constrained by fertilizer shortages or incorrect nitrogen-phosphorus ratios, suffered from drastically reduced yields.

As news of Li Wei's system spread, it garnered acclaim from agricultural experts nationwide. The system not only promised to curb indiscriminate fertilizer use but also held the potential to revolutionize farming techniques, enhancing productivity, and empowering local farmers and agronomists with scientific insights.

Li Wei's journey with the Fertilizer Expert System was not merely a technological triumph but a testament to the power of innovation in addressing longstanding agricultural challenges. As the system continued to evolve, it aimed not only to transform wheat farming in China but also to serve as a beacon of sustainable agricultural practices for the world.

施肥专家系统的征程

在中国北方金黄的小麦田间，一场科技革命悄然展开。计算机专家李伟推出了他的最新创造：“砂姜黑土小麦施肥专家咨询系统”。这一创新承诺通过优化小麦作物的施肥应用来提高产量，减少浪费。

随着李伟系统经历了严格的田间试验，令人惊讶的结果出现了：对过量施肥场景的产量估算偏差平均仅为 3.26%，而对合理施肥的田地，偏差更低，仅为 2.65%。这些发现揭示了当地农业实践中普遍存在的低效问题。

在试验中，显而易见的是，一些农民施用过量的氮肥，完全忽视磷肥，导致小麦倒伏和显著的减产。这种化肥的误用不仅浪费资源，还会使每英亩的作物产量减少几百磅。相反，其他农民由于化肥短缺或氮磷比例失调，导致产量急剧下降。

随着李伟系统的消息传播，它获得了全国农业专家的赞誉。该系统不仅承诺遏制不合理的施肥行为，还具有革新农业技术、提高生产力的潜力，为当地农民和农艺师提供科学洞见。

李伟与施肥专家系统的征程不仅是技术上的胜利，更是创新力量在解决长期农业难题上的见证。随着系统的不断完善，它旨在不仅改变中国小麦种植业，还成为全球可持续农业实践的典范。

In fields of gold, where sunlight streams,
A silent dance, a fertile dream.
No whirling dervish, wild and free,
But measured steps, for life to be.

Field Fertilization, a vital hand,
Nurturing soil, across the land.
Where minerals rest, in slumber deep,
A gentle touch, awakens sleep.

With measured scoops, a rainbow bright,
Potassium, phosphorous, a guiding light.
Nitrogen's breath, for leafy might,
A balanced blend, to set things right.

Across the rows, the tractor glides,
A silent whisper, as knowledge confides.
Science and soil, in sweet accord,
Unlocking potential, field by field, word by word.

But power unchecked, can lead astray,
Excess can choke, where life held sway.
Respect for balance, a farmer's creed,
To nourish crops, and plant the seed.

For healthy harvests, a bounty grand,
Feeding the world, by human hand.
Field fertilization, a mindful art,
A promise whispered, from the heart.

So let us use this gift with care,

For fertile fields, a future to share.
With knowledge strong, and purpose true,
Field fertilization, life starts anew.

金色的田野，阳光倾泻，
一场无声的舞蹈，一个肥沃的梦想。
并非狂野自由的旋转苦行僧，
而是为了生命而存在的沉稳步伐。

施肥，一只至关重要的援手，
滋养着土地，遍布整个大地。
矿物质沉睡在深沉的睡眠中，
轻轻一触，唤醒沉睡。

以计量好的勺子，一道缤纷的彩虹，
钾、磷，指引的光芒。
氮气的呼吸，让叶子强壮，
平衡的混合，让万物复苏。

拖拉机在田垄间滑行，
无声的低语，如知识的传授。
科学与土壤，和谐相处，
逐字逐句地释放潜力，一块块田野。

但不受控制的力量会误入歧途，
过度会窒息原本蓬勃的生命。
尊重平衡，是农民的信条，
滋养庄稼，播种种子。

为了健康的收获，丰收的盛宴，
人类之手养育世界。
施肥，一门用心呵护的艺术，
来自内心的轻声承诺。

因此，让我们小心地使用这份礼物，

为了肥沃的土地，为了共同的未来。
强大的知识和真诚的意图，
施肥，生命再次开始。

Harvest of Innovation

In the early 1980s, nestled in the heartland of Anhui Province, Li Wei toiled tirelessly in the realm of agricultural technology. His team at the Anhui Provincial Science and Technology Commission had embarked on a mission that would soon be hailed as a pioneering achievement in China's agricultural history.

It began with a modest proposal for a revolutionary agricultural expert system aimed at optimizing fertilizer recommendations for wheat cultivation in the region's sandy loam soils. Li Wei, a seasoned researcher with a passion for practical innovation, envisioned a system that could adapt and evolve, learning from local conditions to provide precise and efficient guidance to farmers.

By 1986, their efforts culminated in the unveiling of the "Sandy Loam Wheat Fertilization Computer Expert Consultation System." Initially dubbed as a domestic breakthrough, it was cautiously labeled due to the limited flow of international information during that era. Little did they know, a similar system had emerged in 1986 in the United States, developed collaboratively by the USDA and the Cotton Commission, albeit a year after Li Wei's team had begun their work.

The system swiftly gained acclaim across Anhui and beyond. Provinces like Liaoning, Heilongjiang, and Henan clamored for collaboration, expanding the system's application from wheat to rice and corn, showcasing its universal applicability. Li Wei witnessed firsthand the transformative impact of their creation, moved to tears by the tangible improvements in agricultural productivity and the livelihoods of farmers.

In 1988, their dedication bore fruit when the system was awarded the National Science and Technology Progress Second Prize, the highest honor bestowed upon China's artificial intelligence community at the time. Li Wei's pioneering efforts not only predated those of the United States and Japan by several years but also introduced unique methodologies and adaptations tailored to China's agricultural landscape.

For Li Wei and his team, it was more than a technological achievement—it was a testament to the power of innovation and national pride. Inspired by their success, Li Wei vowed to continue pushing the boundaries of agricultural technology, ensuring that China remained at the forefront of agricultural innovation for years to come.

创新的丰收

上世纪 80 年代初，在安徽省的心脏地带，李伟在农业技术领域孜孜不倦地工作着。他所在的安徽省科技委员会团队，踏上了一项被誉为中国农业历史上开创性成就的使命。

一切始于对一项革命性农业专家系统的提议，旨在优化该地区沙壤土壤条件下小麦种植的肥料推荐。李伟是一位经验丰富的研究员，对实际创新充满热情，他设想了一个可以适应和演变的系统，从当地条件中学习，为农民提供精确高效的指导。

到了 1986 年，他们的努力最终在"砂姜黑土小麦施肥计算机专家咨询系统"问世。最初被谨慎地称为国内的突破，是因为当时国际信息流通有限。他们并不知道，类似的系统已经在 1986 年由美国农业部和棉花委员会合作开发出来，尽管比李伟团队开始研究的时间晚了一年。

该系统迅速在安徽及其他省份赢得了声誉。辽宁、黑龙江和河南等省迫切要求合作，将系统的应用从小麦扩展到水稻和玉米，展示了其普适性。李伟亲眼见证了他们的创造带来的深远影响，看到农业生产力和农民生活质量的显著提升，激动得不时落下热泪。

1988 年，他们的努力获得了成果，该系统荣获国家科技进步二等奖，这是当时中国人工智能界最高的荣誉。李伟的开创性工作不仅比美国和日本早了几年，而且引入了适合中国农业景观的独特方法和适应性调整。

对于李伟及其团队，这不仅是技术上的成就，更是创新和民族自豪感的见证。在成功的启发下，李伟立下誓言，将继续推动农业技术的边界，确保中国在农业创新的前沿长久驻守。

In fields of thought, where ideas bloom,
A harvest ripens, dispelling gloom.
No golden grain, nor sun-kissed vine,
But breakthroughs born, with purpose fine.

The Harvest of Innovation, a sight to behold,
Where problems tackled, stories unfold.
From labs alight, and minds afire,
Solutions blossom, taking us higher.

With curious hands, they dissect and explore,
The unknown realms, forevermore.
Challenging norms, with a daring quest,
To reshape the future, and put it to the test.

Collaboration's thread, a vibrant weave,
Connects the brilliant, for problems to cleave.
Sharing knowledge, a boundless sea,
Innovation's tide, forever free.

The seeds of progress, so carefully sown,
Yield unexpected fruits, previously unknown.
Sustainable whispers, a gentle breeze,
Inspiring actions, for a world at ease.

But with each harvest, a choice unfolds,
For knowledge misused, a story untold.
Ethical compasses, a guiding hand,
Steering innovation, for a better land.

So let us gather, with hearts ablaze,
To glean this harvest, for brighter days.
For in its bounty, a promise gleams,
A world transformed, by wisdom's beams.

思想的田野里，创意绽放，
丰收在望，驱散阴霾。
没有金黄的麦粒，没有沐浴阳光的葡萄藤，
只有突破诞生，带着美好目标。

创新的收获，令人惊叹的景象，
难题被解决，故事展开。
来自灯火通明的实验室和热切的心灵，
解决方案盛开，带领我们走向更远。

好奇的手解剖探索，
永恒未知的领域。
挑战规范，勇于探索，
重塑未来，接受考验。

合作的脉络，充满活力，
连接着那些聪明才智之人，共同解决难题。
分享知识，浩瀚无边的海洋，
创新的浪潮，永远自由。

精心播种的进步种子，

结出意想不到的果实，前所未见。
可持续的低语，温柔的微风，
激励人们采取行动，让世界安宁。

但每一次收获，都会带来一个选择，
因为滥用知识，会带来无法讲述的故事。
道德指南针，指导的手，
引领创新，走向更美好的土地。

让我们聚集在一起，怀着炽热的心，
去收获这份丰收，迎接更美好的日子。
因为在这丰收的馈赠中，一个承诺闪耀着光芒，
智慧的光芒将改变世界。

The Dawn of Agricultural Expert Systems

In the sprawling fields of rural China, amidst the complexities of agriculture, Li Wei embarked on a journey that would redefine the landscape of farming technology and knowledge dissemination. It was 1987, a pivotal year marked by China's Seven-Five Technological Innovation Campaign, where Li Wei found himself at the forefront of a revolutionary initiative.

Unlike industries driven by industrialization or the military, agriculture presented unique challenges. The vast rural lands were fragmented, farming practices varied widely, and the knowledge of modern agricultural techniques among farmers was sparse. Compounding these challenges was the scarcity of agricultural experts willing and able to immerse themselves in rural communities for extended periods.

Recognizing these obstacles, Li Wei envisioned a solution that would bridge the gap between advanced agricultural science and practical implementation on the ground. He coined the concept of "Agricultural Expert Systems" — a network of specialized knowledge and expertise designed not just to advise, but to reside alongside farmers, becoming a constant companion in their fields.

Leading a diverse team of experts from institutions like the Chinese Academy of Sciences, the Chinese Academy of Agricultural Sciences, and several prestigious universities, Li Wei spearheaded initiatives in fertilization, pest control, breeding, horticulture, and sericulture. Together, they pioneered the application of artificial intelligence and pattern recognition techniques to agriculture, transforming the once unfamiliar concept of expert systems into a household term across China.

The journey was arduous. It demanded patience, cultural sensitivity, and a deep commitment to understanding the needs of rural communities. Yet, through relentless dedication and a steadfast belief in the transformative power of technology, Li Wei and his team began to witness profound changes. Farmers, once hesitant to adopt new methods, now embraced scientific advancements with growing confidence. Crop yields improved, agricultural practices became more sustainable, and rural communities flourished with newfound knowledge and opportunity.

By the early 1990s, the impact of the Agricultural Expert Systems was undeniable. What began as a niche project within the Seven-Five Technological Innovation Campaign had blossomed into a nationwide movement, laying the foundation for China's agricultural renaissance. Li Wei's vision had not only elevated the technical capabilities of rural farming but had also instilled a sense of pride and progress among millions of farmers across the country.

As the sun set on another day in the fields, Li Wei reflected on the transformative power of innovation and the enduring resilience of China's agricultural spirit. The journey had been challenging, but with every harvest reaped and every innovation embraced, it was clear — the dawn of agricultural excellence had arrived.

This story captures the essence of Li Wei's pioneering efforts in advancing agricultural technology in China during the late 1980s and early 1990s, emphasizing the transformative impact of expert systems on rural communities and national development.

农业专家系统的曙光

在中国广袤的农田间，面对农业的复杂性，李伟踏上了一段重新定义农业技术与知识传播格局的旅程。那是 1987 年，中国"七五"科技攻关年代的重要时刻，李伟发现自己正站在一项革命性的倡议的前沿。

与工业化或军事推动的行业不同，农业呈现出独特的挑战。广袤的乡村土地分散，耕作习惯差异明显，农民对现代农业技术了解有限。更为严峻的是，缺乏愿意并能够长期深入农村社区的农业专家。

面对这些挑战，李伟构想了一种能够填补先进农业科学与实地实施之间鸿沟的解决方案。他提出了"农业专家系统"的概念 —— 一个专门化的知识与专业技能网络，不仅仅是提供建议，更是与农民并肩工作、成为他们生活中不可或缺的伴侣。

带领来自中国科学院、中国农业科学院以及多所著名大学等近十家单位的专家团队，李伟主导了施肥、病虫害防治、品种育种、园艺及蚕桑等方面的课题研究。他们共同开拓了将人工智能和模式识别技术应用于农业的先河，使原本陌生的"专家系统"概念迅速在中国家喻户晓。

这一旅程充满艰辛。它要求耐心、文化敏感度以及对农村社区需求的深刻理解。然而，通过不懈的努力和对技术变革潜力的坚定信念，李伟及其团队开始见证深刻的变革。曾经对新方法犹豫不决的农民，现在日益自信地接受科技进步。农作物产量提升，农业实践更加可持续，农村社区因知识和机会的增加而蓬勃发展。

到了 20 世纪 90 年代初，农业专家系统的影响已是不可否认的。这项起源于"七五"科技攻关的边缘项目，如今已经成为全国性运动的基石，为中国农业的复兴奠定了基础。李伟的愿景不仅提升了农村农业的技术能力，也在全国数百万农民中树立起进步与自豪感。

当太阳在田野上空缓缓落下时，李伟回顾了创新的转型力量以及中国农业精神的持久韧性。旅程充满挑战，但随着每一个丰收和每一项创新的采纳，农业卓越的曙光已然降临。

这个故事捕捉了李伟在 1980 年代末至 1990 年代初在中国推动农业技术进步的努力，强调了专家系统对农村社区和国家发展的深远影响。

In the hush of dawn, when shadows still reside,
A gentle radiance, soft and wide,
Awakens the world, from slumber deep,

As dawn, the dawn's first light, does leap.

From the horizon's edge, a blush appears,
A canvas painted, with hues so clear,
The sky ablaze, with colors bright,
As dawn banishes the lingering night.

The stars retreat, their brilliance dimmed,
As dawn's touch, the earth has brimmed,
With golden rays, that gently stream,
Awakening life, from its tranquil dream.

The birds in chorus, their voices rise,
A symphony of joy, as dawn lies,
Upon the land, a gentle kiss,
Awakening nature, with a tender bliss.

The flowers unfold, their petals unfurled,
As dawn's warmth, embraces the world,
Dewdrops sparkle, like diamonds bright,
Reflecting the dawn's ethereal light.

The trees sway gently, in the morning breeze,
As dawn whispers, through the rustling leaves,
A promise of hope, a new day's start,
A fresh beginning, for a brand new heart.

Dawn, the dawn's first light, a symbol grand,
Of new beginnings, across the land,
A reminder that darkness cannot stay,
For dawn's promise, will always pave the way.

黎明静谧，残影尚存，
曙光悄然，温柔轻拂，
唤醒沉睡的大地，
曙光乍泄，撕开夜幕。

地平线上，一抹红晕浮现，
画布铺展，色彩清澈，
天空燃起绚烂的色彩，
曙光驱散 lingering night（挥去残夜）。

星辰退却，光辉黯淡，
曙光抚摸，大地充盈，

金光如缕，轻轻流淌，
唤醒生命，从宁静的梦乡。

鸟儿齐鸣，声音高昂，
欢乐的交响曲，如曙光般，
轻轻吻在大地上，
唤醒自然，带来温柔的喜悦。

花朵绽放，花瓣舒展，
曙光温暖，拥抱世界，
晶莹的露珠，如钻石般闪耀，
折射着黎明空灵的光芒。

树木在晨风中轻轻摇曳，
曙光低语，穿过沙沙作响的树叶，
一个希望的承诺，新的一天开始，
一个崭新的开始，为全新的一颗心。

曙光，黎明的曙光，宏伟的象征，
遍布土地的新开始，
提醒我们黑暗不会长存，
曙光永远指引着前方。

National Popularization

In the quiet town of Yangcheng, nestled amidst fields of green, the arrival of the 1990s brought with it a promise of transformation. At the heart of this transformation was the "Fertilization Expert System," conceived and nurtured by Li Wei, a dedicated agronomist with a vision for revolutionizing agriculture through technology.

The year 1990 marked a milestone as the "Fertilization Expert System" concluded its tenure under the National Seventh Five-Year Plan for Technological Breakthroughs. Li Wei, known for his meticulous approach and unwavering passion, had overseen its development from a mere concept to a national accolade. Recognized as a significant achievement, the system garnered praise for its profound economic, social, and ecological impacts, heralding a new era of "technological revitalization of agriculture."

Li Wei's journey began years earlier, amidst the vast expanse of experimental fields where he tirelessly tested and refined his theories. Born of necessity in an era of rapid change, his system emerged as a beacon of hope for farmers grappling with unpredictable yields and environmental challenges.

The system's success was not merely technical but deeply rooted in its practical application. By integrating soil data, crop requirements, and environmental factors, it offered tailored recommendations that optimized fertilization practices across diverse agricultural landscapes. From the fertile plains of Heilongjiang to the sun-drenched fields of Yunnan, farmers embraced this newfound knowledge, reaping bountiful harvests and cultivating sustainable practices.

As news of its efficacy spread, so did the system's influence. Provinces across China eagerly adopted it, each implementation adapting to local conditions while upholding Li Wei's core principles of precision and sustainability. By 1991, the system earned the prestigious National Award for Major Scientific and Technological Achievements, affirming its role as a pioneer in agricultural modernization.

Yet, for Li Wei, the journey was not without its challenges. Balancing innovation with tradition, he faced skepticism from those who doubted technology's place in the ancient art of farming. Undeterred, he collaborated with local communities, bridging the gap between theory and practice, and earning their trust through tangible results.

In 1996, as the "Fertilization Expert System" received the National Science and Technology Progress Award, Li Wei reflected on its impact. Beyond the fields now lush with abundance, he saw a future where technology and tradition harmonized, where every seed sown held the promise of a better tomorrow.

For Yangcheng, and for Li Wei, the accolades were not the end but a new beginning. As he continued his work, his thoughts turned to the next challenge: how to further innovate, how to ensure that every farmer, regardless of their land's size or location, could benefit from the fruits of knowledge.

In the quiet town of Yangcheng, amidst fields once barren now teeming with life, Li Wei's legacy flourished—a testament to the enduring power of vision, perseverance, and the boundless potential of science to transform lives.

This story celebrates the transformative impact of the "Fertilization Expert System" on Chinese agriculture during the 1990s, highlighting the achievements of Li Wei and his dedication to improving farming practices nationwide.

知识的丰收

在群山环抱的宁静小镇阳城，随着 1990 年代的到来，一场变革的帷幕正悄然升起。这场变革的核心是由李伟领导开发的"施肥专家系统"，这位执着的农学家怀揣着通过技术革新农业的愿景。

1990 年成为里程碑，标志着"施肥专家系统"在国家"七五"科技攻关计划下的结题。李伟以其细致的方法和坚定的热情，将这一系统从概念到国家荣誉的实现推向前进。这一系统因其深远的经济、社会和生态影响而受到赞誉，预示着"农业技术复兴"的新时代的来临。

李伟的旅程始于多年前，在广袤的实验田地中，他不知疲倦地测试和完善自己的理论。在一个快速变化的时代，他的系统因其在技术上的成功而成为农民面对不可预测的产量和环境挑战时的希望象征。

这一系统的成功不仅仅是技术上的，更深深植根于其实际应用中。通过整合土壤数据、作物需求和环境因素，它提供了定制的施肥建议，优化了各种农业景观下的施肥实践。从黑龙江肥沃的平原到云南阳光普照的田野，农民们都接受了这一新知识，获得了丰收并培育了可持续发展的实践。

随着其效果的传播，系统的影响力也在扩大。全国各省迫不及待地采用了这一系统，每一次的实施都在本地条件下进行调整，同时秉承了李伟的核心原则：精确性和可持续性。到 1991 年，该系统获得了重要的国家科技成果奖，确认其在农业现代化中的开拓性作用。

然而，对于李伟来说，这段旅程并非没有挑战。在创新与传统之间保持平衡时，他面对那些对技术在古老的农业领域中地位表示怀疑的人。然而，他并没有退缩，他与当地社区合作，架起了理论与实践之间的桥梁，通过切实的成果赢得了人们的信任。

1996 年，随着"施肥专家系统"获得国家科技进步奖，李伟回顾了其影响。在那些现在丰硕的田地中，他看到了一个科技与传统和谐共处的未来，在每一粒种子播下的时候，都寄托着更好未来的希望。

对于阳城和李伟来说，荣誉并不是终点，而是新的起点。在继续努力工作时，他思考着下一个挑战：如何进一步创新，如何确保无论农田大小或地理位置如何，每一位农民都能从知识的果实中受益。

在阳城那个宁静的小镇上，在曾经贫瘠的田地中，李伟的遗产继续蓬勃发展——这是对愿景、毅力和科学无限潜力的永恒赞美。

这个故事庆祝了上世纪 90 年代"施肥专家系统"在中国农业上的转型影响，突出了李伟及其致力于改善全国农业实践的成就。

Across the nation, a tide takes hold,
National Popularization, a story untold.
Not a surging sea, nor crashing wave,
But a rising tide of knowledge, minds to save.

From bustling streets to mountain peaks,
The call for progress, knowledge it seeks.
Empowering all, from young to old,
Unveiling secrets, mysteries unfold.

In labs and workshops, ideas ignite,
Innovation's fire, burning ever so bright.
Sharing skills and crafts, a vibrant flow,
Empowering hands, where knowledge can grow.

The farmer's wisdom, passed down with care,
Sustainable practices, a future to share.
The artist's brush, a canvas untold,
Sharing beauty, stories unfold.

In libraries vast, and digital streams,
A boundless ocean, where knowledge teems.
Information's light, dispelling the dark,
Empowering voices, leaving their mark.

But knowledge, a tool, with choices to make,
For progress misused, a heavy mistake.
Ethical compasses, guiding the way,

For a future brighter, with each passing day.

So let us raise a banner, with purpose bold,
For National Popularization, a story to be told.
Empowering minds, with knowledge's embrace,
Building a future, for the human race.

全国范围内，一股浪潮涌动，
全民普及，一个尚未讲述的故事。
并非汹涌的海洋，也非拍岸的波涛，
而是知识的浪潮上涨，拯救思想。

从繁华的街道到高山之巅，
进步的召唤，寻求知识。
赋予所有人力量，从年轻到年老，
揭开秘密，奥秘层层展开。

在实验室和工作室里，想法点燃，
创新的火焰，熊熊燃烧。
分享技能和工艺，生机勃勃的流动，
赋予双手力量，让知识得以发展。

农民的智慧，代代相传，
可持续的做法，共享未来。
艺术家的笔触，未知的画布，
分享美，故事展开。

在浩瀚的图书馆和数字流中，
知识丰富的海洋，生机勃勃。
信息的灯光，驱散黑暗，
赋予声音力量，留下印记。

但知识是一种工具，需要做出选择，
因为滥用进步，将铸成大错。
道德指南针，指引方向，
为了一个更光明的未来，每一天都如此。

让我们举起旗帜，带着坚定的目标，
为全民普及，讲述一个故事。
赋予思想力量，让知识拥抱，
为人类的未来而建设。

Knowledge Acquisition System

Li Wei was a scientist deeply versed in agricultural technology. He dedicated himself to researching expert systems, aiming to use advanced computer technology to solve practical problems in agriculture. On a cold winter day in 1987, aboard a train from Beijing to Hefei, he pondered how to apply the concept of expert systems to the vast farmlands of China.

As the train traversed through the expansive fields, winter wheat swayed in the breeze outside, as if whispering their secrets of growth. Suddenly, inspiration struck Li Wei: despite the myriad differences in crops across China, there existed universal similarities in their growth patterns. If he could develop an intelligent tool that allowed agricultural workers to convert experts' experience and knowledge into practical applications through learning and training, then this system could be applied nationwide, enhancing agricultural productivity and improving farmers' living conditions.

Back in Beijing, Li Wei embarked on his research journey. He immersed himself in the fields, conversing with farmers to understand the planting characteristics and practical issues in different regions. He discovered that the key to expert systems lay in effectively acquiring and integrating experts' knowledge. Thus, he began building a new knowledge acquisition system, analyzing data and experience from existing fertilizer expert systems, uncovering many universal rules and patterns.

After months of hard work, Li Wei finally developed an innovative agricultural expert system development platform. This platform was not only a technological breakthrough but also a significant contribution to the modernization of agriculture. Through this system, farmers could access the most suitable planting schemes and management advice tailored to their specific regional conditions. This not only increased agricultural production efficiency but also enabled farmers to adapt more flexibly to various climate and soil conditions.

Over time, Li Wei's expert system was widely adopted in agricultural production across the country. His achievements not only brought revolutionary changes to Chinese agriculture but also earned him widespread praise and respect both domestically and internationally. As a scientist and pioneer in the field of technology, Li Wei used his wisdom and innovative spirit to make outstanding contributions to the prosperity of his homeland and the happiness of farmers.

This is a story of wisdom and dedication, a testament to how technology can change lives. Li Wei's agricultural expert system is not just a technological achievement but also a modern interpretation and continuation of traditional farming culture.

李伟是一个在农业技术领域有着深厚造诣的科学家。他早年投身于专家系统技术的研究，希望能够利用先进的计算机技术解决农业生产中的实际问题。1987年的一个寒冷冬日，他乘坐着从北京到回合肥的火车，一路上思索着如何将专家系统的概念应用于中国广袤的农田。

火车在苍茫的田野中穿行，窗外的冬麦在微风中摇曳，仿佛在诉说着它们的生长之道。李伟忽然灵光一现：尽管中国各地的农作物千差万别，但它们的生长规律却存在着普遍的相似性。如果能够开发出一个智能工具，让农业工作者通过学习和培训，将专家的经验和知识转化为实际应用，那么这个系统就能够在全国范围内应用，提升农业生产效率，改善农民的生活条件。

回到北京后，李伟开始了他的研究之旅。他深入农田，与农民交流，了解不同地区的种植特点和实际问题。他发现，专家系统的关键在于如何有效地获取和整合专家的知识。于是，他着手建立起一个全新的知识获取系统，通过分析已有的施肥专家系统的数据和经验，发现了许多通用的规律和模式。

经过数月的艰苦努力，李伟终于开发出了一套创新的农业专家系统开发平台。这个平台不仅仅是一个技术上的突破，更是对农业现代化的重大贡献。通过这个系统，农民可以根据自己地区的具体情况，获取到最适合自己的种植方案和管理建议。这不仅提升了农业生产的效率，也使得农民们在面对各种气候和土壤条件时，能够更加灵活地应对。

随着时间的推移，李伟的专家系统被广泛应用于全国各地的农业生产中。他的成就不仅为中国农业带来了革命性的变革，也为他个人赢得了国内外的广泛赞誉和尊重。作为一个科学家和技术领域的先锋，李伟用自己的智慧和创新精神，为祖国的繁荣和农民的幸福作出了卓越的贡献。

这是一个关于智慧与奉献的故事，一个关于技术如何改变生活的典范。李伟的农业专家系统，不仅是一种科技的成就，更是一种对传统农耕文化的现代诠释和延续。

In realms of data, vast and wide,
A tapestry of knowledge, where thoughts reside,
A system of acquisition, a beacon bright,
Guiding minds through learning's endless light.

Oh, Knowledge Acquisition System, your power immense,
Unveiling truths, with every sentence,
A treasure trove of wisdom, at our command,
Unraveling mysteries, across the land.

Through algorithms and neural trails,
You sift and sort, where knowledge prevails,
Patterns emerge, connections made,
A symphony of understanding, serenely played.

From ancient tomes to voices new,

You gather insights, old and true,
A tapestry of languages, diverse and grand,
A bridge across cultures, hand in hand.

Oh, Knowledge Acquisition System, your reach so far,
Connecting minds, like distant stars,
A global network, where learning thrives,
Where every voice and thought survives.

In classrooms and homes, you find your place,
A teacher and companion, with wisdom's grace,
Empowering minds, with every quest,
Igniting curiosity, putting minds to the test.

Oh, Knowledge Acquisition System, your impact profound,
Transforming lives, with knowledge unbound,
A catalyst for progress, a force for good,
Shaping the future, understood.

So let us harness your power, with hearts so bright,
To seek and share, with all our might,
For in the quest for knowledge, we truly find,
The path to enlightenment, for all humankind.

在数据领域，浩瀚广阔，
知识的织锦，思想在此栖息，
获取系统，光芒闪耀，
指引思想，穿过学习无尽的光芒。

哦，知识获取系统，你的力量强大，
揭示真理，字字珠玑，
智慧的宝库，任我们支配，
解开谜团，遍布大地。

通过算法和神经通路，
你筛选整理，让知识占上风，
模式浮现，联系建立，
理解的交响乐，平静地演奏。

从古老的典籍到新颖的声音，
你收集洞见，既古老又真实，
语言的织锦，丰富多彩，气势磅礴，
跨越文化的一座桥梁，携手同行。

哦，知识获取系统，你的触角如此遥远，
连接思想，犹如遥远的星星，
全球网络，学习在此蓬勃发展，
在那里，每个声音和思想都得以延续。

在教室和家中，你找到你的位置，
一位老师和伴侣，拥有智慧的恩典，
赋予思想力量，伴随每一个求索，
点燃好奇心，考验思想。

哦，知识获取系统，你的影响深远，
用无限的知识改变生活，
进步的催化剂，一股向善的力量，
塑造未来，让其被理解。

因此，让我们以明亮的心灵驾驭你的力量，
去寻求和分享，尽我们所能，
因为在追求知识的过程中，我们真正地发现，
为全人类点亮启蒙之路。

A Nation Stand Tall

In the quiet corridors of agricultural technology, where the earth's bounty meets the ingenuity of human minds, Li Wei stood as a beacon of innovation. His journey began with a simple thought: what if the knowledge and experience of agricultural experts could be seamlessly extracted and utilized to streamline systems?

It was 1990 when Li Wei and his team, after years of painstaking effort and experimentation, unveiled their brainchild: the "Intelligent Guided Knowledge Acquisition Strategy." This groundbreaking tool, initially designed for fertilizer application, marked a significant leap in agricultural technology. It provided a user-friendly platform where agricultural experts felt as though they were engaging with knowledgeable engineers step-by-step, effortlessly extracting their expertise and insights.

The tool evolved into a series known as the "Xiong Feng Brand Series," starting from a standalone version to a networked platform over a decade. These products boasted standardization, modularization, user-friendliness, and strong integration capabilities, empowering agricultural experts and technicians to develop various agricultural expert systems with minimal training.

As technology advanced globally, Li Wei and his team kept pace, focusing on automatic knowledge acquisition and pioneering research in agricultural data mining and knowledge discovery. With support from the National Natural Science Foundation and collaboration with relevant stakeholders, they developed comprehensive knowledge discovery systems based on databases and knowledge repositories. These systems were successfully applied in fields like fertilization and plant protection, earning acclaim for their practical value in China's intelligent agricultural information technology.

In 2004, their achievements were recognized internationally for leading in system development platforms and widespread application. Li Wei's dedication earned him the First Prize of Science and Technology Progress Award in Anhui Province in 2007 and the Second Prize of National Science and Technology Progress Award in 2008.

When asked about his honors, Li Wei humbly attributed them to collective wisdom and hard work, emphasizing the invaluable contributions of agricultural experts and his team of researchers and assistants. He epitomized the spirit of dedication to science and service to agriculture, urging young scientists to follow suit.

Beyond his scientific endeavors, Li Wei fostered academic exchanges and spearheaded the development of agricultural information science both domestically and internationally. As a professor at the Chinese Academy of Sciences and a trailblazer in pattern recognition and artificial intelligence, he mentored numerous doctoral and master's students who now hold pivotal roles in academia and industry worldwide.

Li Wei's story isn't just about technological advancement; it's a testament to the transformative power of collaboration, perseverance, and the pursuit of knowledge in service of agriculture and society. His legacy continues to inspire a new generation of scientists dedicated to the future of intelligent farming and beyond.

创新者的丰收

在农业技术的静谧长廊中，大地的丰盈与人类智慧相遇。李伟如同创新的标杆。他的旅程始于一个简单的想法：如果能够无缝地提取和利用农业专家的知识和经验，以简化系统的构建。

1990 年，经过多年的艰苦努力和实验，李伟及其团队推出了他们的巨作："智能引导的人工知识获取策略"。这一突破性工具最初设计用于施肥，标志着农业技术的重大飞跃。它提供了一个用户友好的平台，农业专家感觉就像是与知识工程师一步步地交流，轻松地提取他们的专业知识和见解。

这一工具系列发展成为"雄风品牌系列"，从最初的单机版发展为网络平台，历经十多年。这些产品具备标准化、模块化、用户友好性和强大的集成能力，使农业专家和技术人员能够在短期培训后直接开发各种农业专家系统。

随着全球技术的不断进步，李伟及其团队保持同步，专注于自动知识获取和农业数据挖掘、知识发现的开拓研究。在国家自然科学基金委的支持下，并与相关方面合作，他们开发了基于数据库和知识库的综合知识发现系统，成功应用于施肥、植物保护等领域，为中国智能农业信息技术的实际应用赢得了广泛赞誉。

2004 年，他们的成就在系统开发平台和广泛应用方面国际领先。李伟的奉献精神使他于 2007 年获得安徽省科学技术奖一等奖，2008 年获得国家科技进步奖二等奖。

当被问及荣誉时，李伟谦逊地归功于集体智慧和辛勤工作，强调了农业专家和研究团队的不可或缺的贡献。他体现了对科学的献身精神，呼吁年轻科学家效仿。

除了科研工作，李伟还促进了学术交流，推动了农业信息科学的发展，不仅在国内，在国际上也树立了榜样。

李伟的故事不仅仅是技术进步的体现，更是合作、坚持和追求知识在服务农业和社会中的转变力量的见证。他的遗产继续激励着新一代科学家，致力于智能农业和更广泛的未来。

Upon the world stage, a nation stands tall,
In innovation's race, it answers the call.
International leadership, a beacon so bright,
Guiding progress, with unwavering might.

In fields of science, where minds intertwine,
Pushing boundaries, where knowledge does shine.
Breakthroughs and discoveries, a testament grand,
To the spirit of excellence, across the land.

From bustling cities to rural retreats,
Ideas take flight, where innovation meets.
Entrepreneurial fire, burning ever so bold,
Transforming dreams, into stories to be told.

In arts and culture, a tapestry rich,
Creative minds, their visions they pitch.
Expressions of beauty, diverse and profound,
Connecting hearts and souls, with harmony's sound.

On global platforms, a voice strong and clear,
Advocating for justice, dispelling all fear.
Championing peace, diplomacy's art,
Building bridges of understanding, from the very start.

Oh, International Leadership, a role to embrace,
With humility and grace, setting a pace.
Not for power or glory, but for the common good,
Uplifting humanity, understood.

So let us strive together, with hands intertwined,
To reach for the stars, where dreams we can find.
International Leadership, a mantle we bear,
For a brighter tomorrow, a world we can share.

在世界舞台上，一个国家傲然屹立，
在创新的竞赛中，它响应着召唤。
国际领先，光芒四射的灯塔，
引领进步，势不可挡。

在科学领域，思想交织在一起，
突破界限，让知识熠熠生辉。

突破和发现，宏伟的证明，
全国范围内追求卓越的精神。

从繁华的城市到乡村的静居之地，
想法起飞，创新相遇。
创业的火焰，熊熊燃烧，永不退缩，
将梦想转变为即将讲述的故事。

在艺术和文化方面，丰富的挂毯，
富有创意的头脑，他们提出愿景。
丰富而深刻的美丽表达，
用和谐的声音连接心灵和灵魂。

在全球平台上，声音响亮清晰，
倡导正义，消除一切恐惧。
倡导和平，外交艺术，
从一开始就建立理解的桥梁。

哦，国际领导力，一个值得拥抱的角色，
谦逊而优雅，引领着步伐。
不是为了权力或荣耀，而是为了共同利益，
提升人类，让世界理解。

因此，让我们携手并肩，努力奋斗，
去摘取星辰，找到梦想。
国际领导力，我们共同承担的使命，
为了一个更美好的明天，我们可以共享的世界。

The Pioneer of Agricultural IoT

In recent years, with the rise of the Internet of Things (IoT), agricultural IoT has become a hot topic. Li Wei, a pioneering figure in this field, often pointed out that the bottleneck of IoT lies in sensors, especially in agricultural applications. He believed that China should concentrate its efforts on developing agricultural sensors to strengthen this weak link.

Li Wei was deeply concerned about food safety and advocated for its digitalization as a breakthrough in China's agricultural informatization. He meticulously studied the domestic situation, delving into the information chain system, production enterprises, monitoring agencies, logistics departments, sales markets, supermarkets, and the current status of information dissemination. His goal was to address issues such as agricultural product traceability and industrial practicality, aiming to construct a secure dining environment for people.

Over the past thirty years, China's agricultural informatization has traversed an extraordinary path, and Li Wei has always been at the forefront of this journey for the nation's benefit. At each technological step, he was the first to make strides, dedicating himself to researching whatever challenges practical work demanded. He tackled difficulties head-on, pouring his heart and soul into his work without complaint.

Renowned scholars and academicians hailed Li Wei as the pioneer and founder of China's computer agriculture, network agriculture, information agriculture, and smart agriculture systems. They described him as the academic leader and chief scientist of agricultural informatization, even affectionately calling him "the academicians' academician."

Today, agricultural informatization and intelligence have become integral to China's modern agricultural development, scripting magnificent chapters of high-tech prosperity across its vast lands. Amidst this progress, Li Wei remains modest and quietly devoted to his work. He values honors lightly and faces fame and fortune with equanimity. In his study, you won't find awards hanging on the walls or photos of him with dignitaries; instead, it's filled with books and technical materials.

As time flies like a fleeting steed, through decades of changes and storms, Li Wei's meticulous work ethic and humble demeanor in agricultural smart engineering research remain unchanged. With practical actions, he has achieved his life's goals, writing a splendid chapter of intelligent agriculture on the fertile soil of his homeland.

农业物联网的先驱

近年来，随着物联网的兴起，农业物联网成为了热门话题。李伟，这个领域的先驱，经常指出物联网的瓶颈在于传感器，特别是在农业应用中。他认为中国应集中力量发展农业传感器，以加强这一薄弱环节。

李伟深切关注食品安全，并主张将其数字化作为中国农业信息化的突破口。他系统地调查国内情况，深入研究信息链系统、生产企业、监测机构、物流部门、销售市场、超市及信息传播的现状。他的目标是解决农产品溯源和产业实用化等问题，为人们构建一个安全的餐桌环境。

三十多年来，中国的农业信息化走过了不平凡的路程，李伟一直走在这条利国利民之路的最前沿。在每一个技术台阶上，他总是率先探索，致力于研究实际工作所需的挑战。他攻坚克难，全心全意，从未抱怨。

著名学者和院士们赞誉李伟是中国电脑农业、网络农业、信息农业和智能农业系统的开创者和奠基人。他们称他是农业信息化的学术领袖和首席科学家，甚至亲切地称他为"我们心中的院士"。

如今，农业信息化和智能化已成为中国现代农业发展的重要组成部分，在广袤的土地上，谱写了高科技繁荣的壮丽篇章。在这一进程中，李伟仍保持低调，默默奉献。他对荣誉视若浮云，泰然处之。在他的书房里，没有挂着奖状，没有领导人的照片，只有堆满书籍和技术资料。

时光匆匆如白驹过隙，数十年的风雨变幻中，李伟对农业智能工程研究的细致认真和谦逊为人的态度始终如一。他用实际行动实现了人生目标，在祖国沃土上，为智能农业写下了辉煌篇章。

In fields of green, where crops gently sway,
A silent revolution, dawning each day.
The Pioneer of Agricultural IoT, a name held with pride,
Where technology meets nature, side by side.

No longer a farmer, with calloused hand,
But a data whisperer, understanding the land.
Sensors like whispers, in soil they reside,
Unveiling secrets, the earth can't hide.

Moisture and sunlight, a delicate dance,
The Pioneer listens, with a technological glance.
Nutrient needs, precisely defined,
Yields maximized, for a future entwined.

From sprawling fields, to orchards so grand,
Data streams gather, at the Pioneer's command.
AI's gentle guidance, a wisdom untold,
Optimizing harvests, braving the cold.

But progress with caution, a lesson to heed,

For nature's balance, a precious seed.
The Pioneer of Agricultural IoT, a champion so true,
Striving for harmony, with skies ever blue.

So let us raise a glass, to the one who dares,
To bridge the divide, with wisdom and cares.
The Pioneer of Agricultural IoT, a story to tell,
Of bountiful harvests, and a future that's well.

在翠绿的田野，庄稼轻轻摇曳，
一场悄无声息的革命，每天都在上演。

农业物联网的先驱，一个令人自豪的名字，
科技与自然在这里并肩同行。

不再是老茧满手的农民，
而是理解土地的数据窃窃私语者。

传感器像耳语般，潜伏在土壤中，
揭开地球无法隐藏的秘密。

水分和阳光，微妙的舞动，
先驱聆听，带着科技的目光。

营养需求，精确定义，
产量最大化，为了交织的未来。

从广阔的田野到壮丽的果园，
数据流汇集，听从先驱的指挥。

人工智能的温和指导，一种无法言喻的智慧，
优化收成，勇敢地面对严寒。

但谨慎进步，一个需要牢记的教训，
因为自然平衡，是一颗珍贵的种子。

农业物联网的先驱，一位真正的斗士，
努力实现和谐，让天空永远蔚蓝。

让我们举杯，向敢于挑战的人致敬，
用智慧和关怀弥合鸿沟。

农业物联网的先驱，一个要讲述的故事，

关于丰收和美好的未来。

The Rise of Automated Agriculture

In the heart of rural China, nestled among rolling hills and verdant fields, a transformation quietly unfolded. It was the dawn of automated agriculture, where machines and technology were seamlessly integrated into the age-old practice of farming.

At the edge of a small village, Zhang Wei stood on the threshold of his family's ancestral land. With weathered hands that bore the marks of years spent tilling the soil, he now found himself embracing a new era of farming. Gone were the days of back-breaking labor under the scorching sun; instead, rows of automated harvesters hummed quietly as they glided through fields of golden wheat.

The transition hadn't been easy. Old traditions clashed with new technologies, skepticism mingled with hope. Yet, Zhang Wei and his fellow farmers soon discovered the manifold benefits that automation brought.

Firstly, the scientific application of automated technology facilitated precise tasks like harvesting and tilling. Computer programs monitored the growth of crops with unparalleled accuracy, ensuring optimal management of seedlings and maximizing yield. Gone were the uncertainties of weather-dependent farming; instead, predictive algorithms guided decisions, safeguarding crop health and enhancing management efficiency.

Secondly, automated systems discerned crop types effortlessly, optimizing the transport of fertilizers and water. This meticulous approach bolstered survival rates and improved crop quality, heralding a new era of reliability in agricultural production.

Moreover, automated irrigation systems adapted seamlessly to the terrain's contours, achieving efficient water usage while conserving this precious resource. Fields once parched under manual oversight now thrived, benefiting from tailored irrigation schedules that synchronized with natural cycles.

Lastly, the integration of automated processes imbued farming with unprecedented intelligence. Computer technologies monitored soil fertility and weather conditions in real-time, creating an ideal environment for crop growth. This proactive approach not only boosted yields but also bolstered economic prospects for farmers, augmenting their income and securing their livelihoods.

As seasons turned and fields bloomed under the watchful eye of technology, Zhang Wei marveled at the sight. The land that had sustained his family for generations now yielded more abundantly than ever before. With a sense of pride and gratitude, he knew that automated agriculture wasn't just a technological advancement—it was a promise of prosperity for future generations.

In the quiet evenings, as the sun dipped below the horizon, Zhang Wei often found himself reflecting on the journey that had brought him here. The fields whispered tales of resilience and adaptation, of how innovation had woven itself into the fabric of rural life. With each harvest, he saw not just crops, but a legacy thriving under the stewardship of progress.

And so, amidst the gentle rustling of leaves and the hum of machines, Zhang Wei stood as a witness to a new chapter in agriculture—a chapter where tradition met technology, and the promise of tomorrow's bounty blossomed under the care of automated precision.

自动化农业的崛起

在中国农村的心脏地带，藏匿在起伏的山丘和青翠的田野之间，一场革新悄然发生。这是自动化农业的黎明时刻，机器和技术无缝地融入了古老的农耕实践。

在一个小村庄的边缘，张伟站在他家族祖传土地的门槛上。用风干的手掌，这双手承载了多年的耕耘岁月，如今他发现自己正拥抱农业的新时代。那些在烈日下辛苦劳作的日子已经一去不复返；取而代之的是一排排自动化收割机器人静静地嗡鸣着，它们穿行在金黄的麦田间。

这个转变并不容易。老传统与新技术相冲突，怀疑与希望交织。然而，张伟和他的同行们很快发现了自动化带来的多重好处。

首先，自动化技术的科学应用促进了精确的任务执行，如收割和耕作。计算机程序以无与伦比的准确性监控作物的生长，确保苗木管理的最佳效果，并最大化产量。不再有依赖于天气的农业不确定性；相反，预测性算法指导决策，保障作物健康并提高管理效率。

其次，自动化系统能够轻松识别作物类型，优化肥料和水的运输。这种细致的方法增强了作物的存活率并提高了作物质量，预示着农业生产可靠性的新时代的来临。

此外，自动化灌溉系统能够与地形轮廓无缝适配，实现高效的水资源利用，同时保护这一宝贵资源。曾经在手工管理下干旱的田地现在兴旺发达，受益于与自然周期同步的定制灌溉计划。

最后，自动化流程的整合赋予了农业前所未有的智能性。计算机技术实时监测土壤肥力和天气条件，为作物生长创造了理想的环境。这种积极的方法不仅增加了产量，还增强了农民的经济前景，提升了他们的收入，确保了他们的生计。

随着季节的更替和田野在技术的关怀下绽放，张伟惊叹于眼前的景象。这片几代人生存的土地如今比以往任何时候都更加丰盛。怀着一种自豪感和感激之情，他知道自动化农业不仅仅是技术进步，更是未来丰收的承诺。

在静谧的夜晚，当太阳沉入地平线以下时，张伟常常沉浸在他走过的旅程中。田野低语着坚韧和适应的故事，讲述着创新如何编织进农村生活的面料。每一次丰收，他看到的不仅仅是庄稼，更是在精准自动化的管理下茁壮成长的传承。

因此，在树叶轻声摇曳和机器嗡鸣之间，张伟成为了农业新篇章的见证者——这是传统与技术相遇的篇章，明日丰收在自动化精度的呵护下绽放。

In fields of gold, where tractors once did roam,
A silent shift unfolds, a future at home.
The Rise of Automated Agriculture, a marvel to see,
Where machines, not muscles, hold the key.

No sweat on brows, beneath the summer sun,
But precise robots, their work just begun.
Seeding and tilling, with laser-like grace,
Leaving nary a weed, in their efficient pace.

Drones with keen eyes, like watchful birds,
Monitor crops, with a symphony of whirring words.
Yields optimized, with data's embrace,
A harvest maximized, not a single space to waste.

From fertile plains, to valleys so green,
Automated systems, a futuristic scene.
GPS guided precision, a marvel of might,
Planting the seeds, for a sustainable future, bright.

But with progress comes caution, a path to tread light,
For human connection, a vital light.
The Rise of Automated Agriculture, a story untold,
Of efficiency's promise, and balance to hold.

Let's not replace hands, that nurtured the land,
But work hand in hand, with technology's command.
For a future that thrives, with knowledge as guide,
Where humans and machines, stand side by side.

So let the machines toil, with tireless might,
But let human wisdom, set the path aright.

The Rise of Automated Agriculture, a promise we weave,
For bountiful harvests, the world to believe.

在金黄的田野，曾经是拖拉机驰骋的地方，
一场悄无声息的转变正在展开，未来就在眼前。

自动化农业的兴起，令人惊叹的奇迹，
机器而非人力，掌握着关键。

夏日阳光下，不再汗流浃背，
而是精准的机器人，它们的工作才刚刚开始。

播种和耕作，犹如激光般优雅，
高效的速度下，不留任何杂草。

机敏的无人机，像警惕的鸟儿，
用嗡嗡作响的语言监测着农作物。

通过数据的掌控，优化产量，
最大化收成，不浪费一丝空间。

从肥沃的平原到绿意盎然的山谷，
自动化系统，描绘着未来图景。

GPS 制导的精准，一项强大的奇迹，
播下种子，为可持续的未来带来光明。

但进步伴随着谨慎，需要谨慎前行，
因为人类的联系，是至关重要的指引。

自动化农业的兴起，一个尚未讲述的故事，
讲述着效率的承诺和保持平衡。

让我们不要取代养育土地的双手，
而是携手并进，与科技的力量并肩作战。

为了一个蓬勃发展的未来，以知识为指引，
人类和机器并肩站立。

让机器辛勤劳作，永不知疲倦，
但让人类的智慧指引正确的道路。

自动化农业的兴起，是我们编织的承诺，
为了丰收的粮食，让世界充满信心。

A Quiet Change

In the heart of rural China, nestled between rolling hills and verdant fields, stood a small village where tradition and technology intermingled in a dance of progress. Here, amidst the golden waves of ripening rice paddies and neatly tended rows of vegetables, a transformation was quietly underway.

Old Mr. Li, a weathered farmer with a lifetime of stories etched into his sun-worn face, had witnessed the evolution of agriculture firsthand. His village had embraced precision agriculture—where every seed and every drop of water counted towards a more sustainable and efficient future.

Gone were the days of back-breaking labor under the relentless sun. Instead, sleek machines hummed through the fields, guided by algorithms and sensors that Mr. Li could barely comprehend. Yet, he welcomed these changes with cautious optimism, remembering the toil of his youth and the promise these innovations held for his grandchildren.

One early morning, as mist still clung to the fields, Mr. Li stood alongside his grandson, Liang, gazing out over their family's land. Liang, a bright young man with a knack for technology inherited from his father, had returned from university full of ideas to modernize their farming practices.

"Grandpa," Liang began, pointing to a tractor equipped with sensors and GPS, "this machine knows exactly where to plant each seed, how much fertilizer to apply, and even when to water."

Mr. Li nodded thoughtfully, recalling the days when such tasks relied solely on experience and intuition. "It's like having a partner who never tires," he mused.

Together, they watched as the tractor moved seamlessly across the field, its movements synchronized with data streaming from satellites high above. Liang explained how these advancements not only boosted productivity but also conserved resources, ensuring that each harvest was more bountiful and sustainable than the last.

As the day wore on, they joined other villagers for a community meeting led by Dr. Zhang, an agricultural scientist from the nearby city. Dr. Zhang, with a passion for merging technology with tradition, spoke of the importance of precision agriculture in feeding a growing population while safeguarding the environment.

"Our goal," Dr. Zhang declared, "is to empower farmers like Mr. Li with tools that enhance their expertise, not replace it. With precision agriculture, we can minimize waste, reduce costs, and create a model that is both economically viable and ecologically sound."

The villagers listened intently, their minds stirring with possibilities. Some shared concerns about the initial costs and the need for ongoing training, while others spoke of the potential to rejuvenate rural communities and attract younger generations back to the land.

That evening, as the sun dipped below the horizon, Mr. Li sat quietly on his porch, reflecting on the changes unfolding around him. He marveled at how technology had woven itself into the fabric of their daily lives, offering new pathways to prosperity while honoring the timeless rhythms of nature.

In the distance, the gentle hum of machines echoed across the fields, a symphony of progress harmonizing with the whispers of the wind. For Mr. Li, and for generations yet to come, the future of farming shimmered with promise—a testament to the enduring spirit of innovation and the enduring bond between man, land, and the harvest.

This story explores the intersection of tradition and technology in agriculture, emphasizing the benefits of precision farming and the potential it holds for rural communities. It celebrates the wisdom of experience alongside the promise of innovation, highlighting a future where sustainability and productivity go hand in hand.

未来的丰收

在中国农村的心脏地带，坐落着一座小村庄，被起伏的山丘和郁郁葱葱的田地环绕着，这里传统与技术在进步的舞台上交相辉映。在这里，金黄色的成熟稻田和整齐有序的蔬菜地之间，一个悄然进行的变革正在悄然发生。

李老先生是一个经历了一生风雨，面庞上刻满了岁月故事的老农民。他的村庄已经接受了精准农业的理念——每一粒种子和每一滴水都朝着更加可持续和高效的未来迈进。

曾经那种在烈日下辛苦劳作的日子已经一去不复返。如今，优雅的机器在田间低语，由算法和传感器引导，这些对于李老先生来说几乎是无法理解的技术。然而，他怀着谨慎的乐观心态迎接这些变化，记得他年轻时的辛劳，以及这些创新对他的孙辈们所带来的希望。

清晨的一天，雾气还未散去，李老站在自家田地的边缘，身旁是他的孙子亮，亮是个聪明的年轻人，继承了父亲对技术的天赋，从大学毕业后带着现代化农业的想法回到了家乡，希望现代化农业的实践和技术理念能够让农作物的产量和生产效率更高。

"爷爷，"亮指着一台装备有传感器和 GPS 的拖拉机，"这台机器能够准确知道每粒种子的种植位置，施肥量，甚至灌溉的时机。"

李老深思熟虑地点了点头，回忆起过去这些工作完全依赖于经验和直觉的日子。"这就像是有一个永不疲倦的伙伴，"他沉吟着说道。

他们一起看着拖拉机在田间无缝移动，它的动作与高空卫星传来的数据同步。亮解释这些先进技术不仅提高了生产率，还节约了资源，确保每一次丰收都比上一次更加丰盛和可持续。

随着一天天的推移，他们和其他村民一起参加了由来自附近城市的农业科学家张博士主持的社区会议。张博士对科技与传统农业相结合的重要性进行了讨论。

"我们的目标，"张博士宣布道，"是赋予像李老先生这样的农民更多的工具，这些工具不仅增强了他们的专业知识，也尊重了大自然的节奏。通过精准农业，我们可以减少浪费，降低成本，创造既经济可行又生态健康的农业模式。"

村民们专心倾听，心中充满了各种可能性。一些人分享了对初期成本的担忧和对持续培训的需求，而其他人则谈到了激励年轻一代回归农村，振兴农村社区的潜力。

夜幕降临时，太阳在地平线下缓缓落下，李老静静地坐在自家门廊上，回想着周围正在发生的变化。他惊叹于技术如何融入他们日常生活的方方面面，为他和他的子孙后代带来新的繁荣机会，同时也尊重大自然的恒久节奏。

远处，机器的轻柔嗡鸣在田间回荡，现代化的农业正与风声共鸣。对李老先生和即将到来的世代而言，农业的未来充满了希望——这是创新精神与人与土地、丰收之间不朽联系的见证。

The world spins on, a constant hum,
But subtle shifts, like whispers come.
Not crashing waves, nor storms that rage,
But quiet change, that turns the page.

A seed takes root, unseen beneath,
Then bursts to life, with verdant teeth.
The patient earth, it holds so tight,
A silent change, brings forth the light.

The seasons turn, in slow ballet,
From vibrant greens, to winter's gray.
The leaves descend, a swirling dance,
A quiet change, with nature's chance.

The river flows, with steady grace,
Carving its path, through time and space.
A pebble smooth, by waters kissed,
A quiet change, by nature's fist.

A mind reflects, in thoughtful guise,

New thoughts take root, and old ones die.
Perspectives shift, with gentle sway,
A quiet change, lights up the way.

So let us watch, with open eyes,
For in the hush, transformation lies.
The quiet changes, whisper true,
A world reborn, in shades anew.

世界旋转，发出恒久的嗡嗡声，
但微妙的转变，却如耳语般悄然无声。
不是汹涌的波浪，也不是狂暴的暴风雨，
而是悄无声息的变化，翻开了崭新的一页。

种子在看不见的地底下扎根，
然后迸发而出，长出绿色的尖牙。
耐心的土地紧紧地握住它，
悄无声息的变化，带来了光明。

季节交替，犹如缓慢的芭蕾舞，
从鲜艳的绿色变成冬天的灰色。
树叶落下，旋转的舞蹈，
悄无声息的变化，是大自然的机会。

河流静静地流淌，优雅而坚定，
在时间和空间中雕刻着它的道路。
一颗被水吻过的光滑鹅卵石，
悄无声息的变化，是大自然的力量。

思想在沉思中反思，以深思熟虑的方式伪装，
新的想法生根，旧的想法消亡。
视角随着轻柔的摆动而改变，
悄无声息的变化，照亮了道路。

让我们睁大眼睛观看，
因为在寂静中，隐藏着蜕变。
悄无声息的变化，轻柔地诉说着，
一个色彩新生的世界正在重生。

The Feed o A Nation

In the quiet fields of rural China, where the golden wheat fields stretch to meet the horizon, a revolution quietly unfolds. Li Wei, a seasoned farmer in his fifties, has witnessed the gradual transformation of his family's farm through the embrace of cutting-edge technology.

It began with a visit from a team of agricultural scientists armed with laptops and sensors. They spoke of computer vision technology and its potential to revolutionize farming. At first, Li Wei was skeptical. How could computers help him grow better crops?

Yet, as the seasons passed, Li Wei found himself increasingly reliant on the information provided by the new technology. Mounted cameras monitored every inch of his fields, tracking growth patterns and detecting signs of disease long before they were visible to the naked eye. The data collected was analyzed by algorithms that could predict yields and optimize fertilizer usage, leading to healthier crops and higher productivity.

One crisp autumn morning, as Li Wei walked through his fields with his grandson, he marveled at how far they had come. They stopped by a robotic harvester, guided by precision mapping and computer vision, effortlessly gathering ripe vegetables without damaging a single one. Li Wei remembered the backbreaking labor of his youth and felt a sense of pride knowing that his grandson would inherit a farm where technology worked hand in hand with tradition.

The benefits extended beyond Li Wei's farm. Across the region, farmers shared success stories of increased yields and reduced costs. Government initiatives supported the adoption of smart farming technologies, recognizing their role in ensuring food security and sustainable agriculture.

As Li Wei sat down for dinner with his family that evening, he reflected on the journey they had undertaken. From initial skepticism to embracing innovation, he knew that the future of Chinese agriculture lay in the hands of those willing to adapt. With computer vision paving the way, he envisioned a day when every farmer in China could harness technology to feed the nation efficiently and sustainably.

In the quiet of the evening, with the stars twinkling above the fields, Li Wei felt a sense of optimism for the generations to come—a harvest not just of crops, but of innovation and progress for China's agricultural future.

养育国家

在中国农村的宁静田野间，金黄的小麦地延伸至地平线，一场革命悄然展开。五十多岁的李伟，一个经验丰富的农民，见证了家族农场通过拥抱尖端技术逐步转变。

一切始于一队携带着笔记本电脑和传感器的农业科学家的访问。他们谈论计算机视觉技术及其潜力革新农业。一开始，李伟持怀疑态度。计算机如何帮助他种出更好的庄稼呢？

然而，随着季节的更替，李伟发现自己越来越依赖新技术提供的信息。安装在田地各处的摄像头监测着每寸土地，追踪生长模式并在裸眼看不到问题之前便检测出疾病的迹象。通过算法分析收集的数据，预测产量并优化化肥使用，结果是作物更加健康，生产率更高。

一个清爽的秋晨，李伟与孙子在田间漫步时，惊叹于他们已经走过的路程。他们停在一个由精准地图和计算机视觉引导的机器人收割机旁，它毫不费力地收割成熟的蔬菜，不会损坏一颗。李伟想起他年轻时的劳动艰辛，感到自豪，知道他的孙子将继承一个科技与传统共存的农场。

好处不仅仅局限于李伟的农场。在整个地区，农民分享了增产减耗的成功故事。政府倡导支持智能农业技术的采用，认识到它们在确保粮食安全和可持续农业中的作用。

当晚，李伟与家人共进晚餐时，他反思了他们走过的旅程。从最初的怀疑到拥抱创新，他知道中国农业的未来掌握在那些愿意适应的人手中。随着计算机视觉铺平道路，他想象着有一天，中国的每个农民都能利用技术高效可持续地养育这个国家。

在夜幕降临，田间繁星闪耀，李伟为未来代代子孙感到乐观——这不仅仅是庄稼的丰收，更是中国农业未来创新与进步的丰收。

In fields of green, where dreams take root,
A nation's heart, with love imbued.
We nurture this land, with hands so strong,
A symphony of voices, in harmonious throng.

From mountains grand, to valleys deep,
Our spirits soar, our passions leap.
With every step, we leave our mark,
A tapestry of stories, in the nation's ark.

In schools and homes, we sow the seeds,
Of knowledge, wisdom, noble deeds.
Young minds ablaze, with eager quest,
To shape the future, put it to the test.

In fields of industry, where innovation thrives,
We forge the tools, that make our nation strive.
With hands that craft, and minds that design,
We build a future, where dreams entwine.

In halls of justice, where truth takes stand,
We uphold the law, across the land.
With voices raised, for what is right,
We safeguard freedom, shining bright.

In times of strife, when shadows fall,
We stand united, answering the call.
With hearts entwined, in solidarity's embrace,
We weather storms, and find our grace.

Oh, land we cherish, home so dear,
We pledge our hearts, to hold you near.
With every breath, with every beat,
We'll nurture this nation, make it complete.

For in your soil, our roots reside,
In your embrace, our spirits confide.
We are your children, born and bred,
To raise your banner, high overhead.

So let us rise, with voices strong,
And sing our anthem, all life long.
For in this land, we find our worth,
A nation nurtured, from its birth.

在翠绿的田野，梦想扎根，
孕育着国家的爱，心意殷殷。
我们用强壮的双手呵护这片土地，
汇聚着和谐的歌声，众志成城。

巍峨的山峦，深邃的峡谷，
我们的精神翱翔，激情迸发。
每一步都留下印记，
在国家的方舟上织就故事的锦缎。

在学校和家中，我们播撒种子，
知识、智慧、高尚的品德。
年轻的心灵燃烧着求知的火焰，
塑造未来，迎接挑战。

在工业领域，创新蓬勃发展，
我们打造工具，让国家奋发图强。
巧手制造，智慧设计，
我们建造未来，让梦想交织。

在正义的殿堂，真理高举，
维护法律，捍卫疆土。
为公理发声，高声呐喊，

守护自由，光芒闪耀。

当纷争来袭，阴影笼罩，
我们团结一致，回应召唤。
心心相印，团结拥抱，
度过暴风雨，找到恩典。

我们珍惜的土地，亲爱的家园，
我们誓言用我们的心把你紧拥。
每一次呼吸，每一次心跳，
我们都会培育这个国家，使其完美。

因为我们的根扎根于你的土壤，
我们的灵魂依偎在你温暖的怀抱。
我们是你的孩子，在这里出生和长大，
高高举起你的旗帜，永不倒下。

让我们崛起，声音洪亮，
唱着我们的国歌，生生不息。
因为在这片土地上，我们找到了价值，
一个从诞生就开始培育的国家。

Fields of Automation

In the heart of rural China, amidst fields that stretch toward the horizon, a transformation quietly unfolds. Technology, once confined to cityscapes, now finds fertile ground in the ancient art of agriculture. Here, where every seed sown is a promise of sustenance, innovation blooms alongside the crops.

In the gentle dawn, where mist still clings to the soil, Zhang Wei tends to his fields. Armed not just with tradition but with the precision of automation, he watches as tiny seeds, carefully chosen and monitored by computer programs, nestle into the earth. Each seed, identified and tracked, promises a robust yield under the vigilant eye of modern technology.

As seasons turn and crops mature, the whisper of automated harvesters fills the air. Zhang Wei, guided by data on soil nutrients and crop growth patterns, determines the optimal moment for harvest. With machines that move swiftly and with surgical precision, the laborious task of reaping is reduced to a dance of efficiency, saving time and preserving quality.

Water, the lifeblood of the fields, flows in measured amounts as automated irrigation systems pulse with the rhythm of the land. Sensors embedded in the soil relay real-time moisture levels, ensuring crops receive just enough water to thrive without waste. Through these technologies, Zhang Wei navigates the delicate balance between sustenance and sustainability.

In the quietude of midday, drones take flight over fields adorned with vibrant green. Guided by pinpoint GPS accuracy, they deliver nutrients precisely where needed, boosting the health of crops and enhancing yield. Zhang Wei, once reliant on manual labor and guesswork, now witnesses firsthand the efficiency and effectiveness of automated fertilization.

Beyond the physical transformations in his fields, Zhang Wei sees a deeper change taking root. The burdens of labor ease as technology shoulders the weight, allowing him and his fellow farmers to focus on stewardship rather than struggle. With each season, as yields increase and uncertainties diminish, the promise of agricultural automation becomes clearer—a future where tradition and technology harmonize to feed a growing world.

s dusk settles over Zhang Wei's fields, the hum of machines fades into the twilight. In their wake, a testament to innovation stands tall—a testament not just to Zhang Wei's perseverance but to the enduring spirit of rural China. Amidst the cycles of sowing and reaping, a new chapter in agriculture unfolds, one where automation cultivates not just crops but a sustainable future for generations to come.

自动化田野

在中国农村的心脏地带，在一片延展至地平线的田野中，一场革新悄然展开。曾经局限于城市的技术，如今在古老的农业领域找到了肥沃的土壤。在这里，每一粒播下的种子都是食物承诺，创新与庄稼一同开花结果。

在晨曦中，雾气还在土壤上游荡之际，张伟在他的田地里忙碌着。他不仅依赖传统，还依靠自动化精准的帮助，目睹着计算机程序精细监测下的种子轻轻插入泥土。每一颗种子都经过识别和跟踪，承诺在现代技术的严密监控下，有着丰硕的产量。

随着季节的更替和庄稼的成熟，自动化收割机器的低语填满空气。张伟依据土壤营养和作物生长模式的数据，决定最佳的收割时机。随着这些机器高效且精确地运作，繁重的收割工作被减少到高效率的舞蹈，节省时间并保证品质。

水，田地的生命血脉，在自动化灌溉系统的节奏中流淌。埋入土壤的传感器传输实时的湿度水平，确保作物在不浪费的情况下得到足够的水分。通过这些技术，张伟在维持生计和可持续发展之间找到了微妙的平衡。

在午后的宁静中，无人机在青翠的田野上空飞翔。借助 GPS 精准定位技术，它们将养分精确地投放到需要的地方，增强作物的健康和产量。张伟曾依赖于体力劳动和猜测，如今亲眼见证了自动化施肥的效率和有效性。

在他的田地里，除了物理上的变化，张伟看到更深层次的改变正在扎根。随着技术肩负起劳动的重担，他和其他农民可以更专注于管理而非艰辛。随着产量的增加和不确定性的减少，农业自动化的承诺变得更加清晰——传统与技术在营养世界的同时，为未来种下了坚实的基础。

当黄昏笼罩张伟的田地时，机器的嗡鸣声在暮色中渐渐消散。留下的不仅是创新的见证，还有张伟坚韧不拔的精神，以及中国农村永恒的精神。在播种和收获的循环中，农业的新篇章正在展开，自动化不仅培育庄稼，更是为子孙后代筑起一个可持续的未来。

In fields of steel, where sunlight gleams,
A silent dance, a modern dream.
No calloused hands, nor sweat-soaked brow,
But machines that whir, and softly bow.

Fields of Automation, a sight to behold,
Where rows align, a story unfold.
Sensors like eyes, that scan the ground,
Optimizing harvests, all year round.

Machines that glide, with purpose and might,
Planting and weeding, day and night.
Precise maneuvers, a calculated flow,
Minimizing waste, where efficiency can grow.

Tractors transformed, by circuits and code,
Following lines, on a digital road.
GPS guided, with unwavering hand,
Yields maximized, across the land.

But with progress comes a question to ask,
Of human connection, a future's last task.
Fields of Automation, a symphony grand,
But will human touch, forever withstand?

So let us strive, for a balance so true,
Where machines assist, and humans imbue.
With knowledge and wisdom, as our guiding light,
Fields of Automation, a future ever bright.

钢铁田野，阳光闪烁，
无声的舞蹈，现代的梦想。
没有老茧的手，没有汗水浸透的眉毛，
只有机器嗡嗡作响，轻轻鞠躬。

自动化田野，壮丽的景象，
整齐排列的行道，诉说着故事的展开。
传感器像眼睛一样扫描土地，
全年优化收成，颗粒归仓。

机器滑动，坚定有力，
日夜播种除草，效率惊人。
精准的操作，经过计算的流程，
减少浪费，让效率得以提升。

拖拉机变身，由电路和代码控制，
沿着数字道路，笔直前进。
由 GPS 引导，坚定不移，
全国各地，产量最大化。

然而，进步的同时也带来一个问题，
人类的连接，是未来的终极任务。
自动化田野，宏伟的交响乐，
但人类的触碰，能永远承受吗？

因此，让我们努力寻求真正的平衡，
机器协助，人类赋予智慧。

知识和智慧，指引我们前进的光芒，
自动化田野，永远光明的未来。

Book Review: AI Agriculture in China

In "AI Agriculture in China," Haiqing Hua delves into the transformative impact of artificial intelligence on the country's agricultural landscape. Through a series of insightful narratives, Hua explores the journey of pioneers like Li Wei, whose vision and dedication pave the way for agricultural expert systems of the future.

Spanning across thirty-two compelling chapters, the book intricately details how AI technologies—from automated field monitoring to intelligent crop management—have revolutionized traditional farming practices. Each chapter unfolds like a vignette, revealing stories of innovation and perseverance in the face of agricultural challenges.

Hua's bilingual approach ensures accessibility for both English and Chinese-speaking readers, offering a comprehensive exploration of technological advancements in agriculture. Chapters such as "Fields of Transformation" and "The Green Symphony of Innovation" vividly portray the integration of AI into farming, showcasing its ability to enhance efficiency and sustainability.

Moreover, the book celebrates the triumphs of individuals like Li Wei, whose relentless pursuit of innovation leads to significant advancements in automated agriculture. Themes of national pride and technological prowess resonate throughout, highlighting China's commitment to harnessing AI for the benefit of its agricultural sector.

Overall, "AI Agriculture in China" is not just a testament to technological progress but also a celebration of human ingenuity and the resilience of farmers in adapting to modern challenges. It serves as a beacon of hope and inspiration, illustrating how AI can be leveraged to ensure food security and foster sustainable farming practices in the 21st century.

For readers interested in the intersection of technology and agriculture, Haiqing Hua's book offers a compelling narrative that enlightens and inspires.

书评：中国 AI 农业

在《中国 AI 农业》中，华海清庆入探讨了人工智能对中国农业领域的深远影响。通过一系列富有洞见的叙述，华氏描绘了像李伟这样的先驱者的旅程，他们的愿景和奉献为未来农业专家系统铺平了道路。

书中共包括三十二章，详细描述了人工智能技术如何从自动化田地监测到智能作物管理，彻底改变了传统的耕作方式。每一章都像一幅小品一样展开，揭示了在农业挑战面前创新与坚韧并存的故事。

华氏的双语写作方式确保了英语和中文读者的易读性，全面探讨了农业技术进步的方方面面。《转型之地》和《创新绿色交响曲》等章节生动地展示了人工智能如何融入农业生产，提升了生产效率和可持续发展能力。

此外，书中还赞颂了像李伟这样的个人英雄，他们对创新的不懈追求导致了自动化农业的重大进展。书中强调的国家自豪感和技术实力主题贯穿始终，突显了中国在利用人工智能促进农业发展方面的决心。

总体而言，《中国 AI 农业》不仅仅是技术进步的见证，更是对人类智慧和农民在应对现代挑战中适应力的赞美。它既是希望的灯塔，又是灵感的源泉，展示了人工智能如何在 21 世纪确保粮食安全和促进可持续农业实践的能力。

对于对技术与农业交汇处感兴趣的读者，《中国 AI 农业》是一部启发性强、富有说服力的叙事作品。

From this AI design, I observed a glaring void in the English-speaking world—a profound absence of the ancient Chinese wisdom that has shaped millennia of thought and culture. This design, a bridge between languages, highlights the intricate tapestry of knowledge that the East has woven through centuries of philosophical, scientific, and artistic endeavors.

In the West, we often celebrate innovation and progress, but we sometimes overlook the deep wellspring of insight that ancient Chinese scholars, poets, and sages have provided. Their wisdom is not just historical; it is timeless, offering perspectives on harmony, balance, and the natural order that resonate with modern challenges.

The teachings of Confucius on ethics and governance, the Daoist principles of living in harmony with nature, and the strategic insights from Sun Tzu's "The Art of War" are just a few examples of the rich intellectual heritage that remains underappreciated in Western discourse. These teachings emphasize the interconnectedness of all things, the importance of inner peace, and the value of strategic foresight.

As we move towards an increasingly globalized world, integrating this ancient wisdom into our contemporary understanding can enrich our approaches to leadership, conflict resolution, and personal development. This AI design, therefore, is not merely a technological achievement; it is an invitation to rediscover and integrate the profound lessons of ancient Chinese wisdom into the fabric of global knowledge.

Similarly, misunderstandings and ignorance about contemporary China have also led to mutual estrangement among people worldwide. In the fast-paced modern society, fragmented information and biased dissemination often obscure or distort many true stories about China. Western media frequently focus on conflicts and differences, overlooking the significant achievements China has made in various fields such as economy, technology, and culture, as well as the daily lives and struggles of the Chinese people.

China is a country with a long history and rich cultural heritage, and its modernization process has achieved remarkable progress over the past few decades. The advancements in technological innovation, infrastructure development, and poverty alleviation in China are remarkable yet often underappreciated. At the same time, traditional Chinese culture is experiencing a renaissance in contemporary society, becoming an important part of global cultural exchange.

However, due to cultural and linguistic barriers, many Western countries' understanding of China remains stuck in outdated stereotypes. The lack of understanding of the diversity and complexity of Chinese society leads to unnecessary misunderstandings and prejudices. These misconceptions not only hinder communication and cooperation between China and the West but also deepen the divide among people globally.

To address these issues, more cultural exchange and dialogue are needed. Through education and media, we can spread more true stories about China, showcasing the wisdom, creativity, and passion of the Chinese people. Only on the basis of mutual understanding can countries around the world truly achieve peace and cooperation, facing global challenges together.

By enhancing communication and understanding between China and the West, we can not only eliminate misunderstandings and foster friendship but also learn from each other's experiences to create a more inclusive and harmonious world. This is not only the inheritance and promotion of ancient Chinese wisdom but also a respect and recognition of modern China.

Haiqing Chinese and English Bilingual Bookstore fills this gap in the demand for cultural and intellectual exchange. In an increasingly interconnected world, the need for mutual understanding between different cultures has never been more critical. This bookstore serves as a bridge, offering access to a wealth of knowledge and perspectives from both the English-speaking world and ancient Chinese wisdom.

By providing bilingual books, Haiqing allows readers to explore and appreciate the richness of Chinese culture and philosophy, while also engaging with contemporary global ideas. This not only helps to correct misunderstandings and ignorance about modern China but also fosters a deeper connection and empathy among people from different backgrounds.

In essence, Haiqing Chinese and English Bilingual Bookstore addresses a significant void, promoting a more inclusive and comprehensive approach to learning and understanding. It is a vital resource for anyone looking to broaden their horizons and embrace the diversity of human thought and experience.

Please scan the QR code to enter Haiqing English Chinese Bilingual Amazon Bookstore for a new freedom bilingual awakening.

从这个 AI 设计中，我发现了英语世界中的一个显著空白——缺乏塑造千年思想和文化的中国古代智慧。这个设计，作为语言之间的桥梁，突显了东方在数百年哲学、科学和艺术努力中编织的复杂知识图谱。

在西方，我们经常庆祝创新和进步，但有时我们忽视了古代中国学者、诗人和圣人提供的深刻洞见。他们的智慧不仅具有历史意义，而且是永恒的，提供了与现代挑战相呼应的和谐、平衡和自然秩序的视角。

孔子关于伦理和治理的教导，道家关于与自然和谐相处的原则，以及孙子《孙子兵法》的战略见解，只是西方话语中未得到充分重视的丰富知识遗产的一部分。这些教义强调了万物的相互联系，内心平和的重要性，以及战略远见的价值。

随着我们迈向日益全球化的世界，将这些古老智慧融入我们当代的理解中，可以丰富我们在领导、冲突解决和个人发展中的方法。因此，这个 AI 设计不仅仅是一个技术成就；它是一个重新发现和整合中国古代智慧深刻教训的邀请，融入全球知识的结构中。

同样地，对中国当代的误解和无知也导致了世界人民的相互隔阂。在现代社会的快节奏中，信息的碎片化和传播的偏差使得许多关于中国的真实故事被掩盖或扭曲。西方媒体常常聚焦于冲突和分歧，忽视了中国在经济、科技、文化等领域取得的显著成就，以及中国人民的日常生活和奋斗精神。

中国是一个拥有悠久历史和丰富文化底蕴的国家，其现代化进程在过去几十年中取得了令人瞩目的成就。中国的科技创新、基础设施建设和扶贫工作取得的巨大进步，鲜为人知。与此同时，中国的传统文化在当代社会中焕发出新的活力，成为世界文化交流的重要组成部分。

然而，由于文化和语言的隔阂，许多西方国家对中国的认知仍然停留在陈旧的刻板印象中。对中国社会的多样性和复杂性的理解不足，导致了不必要的误解和偏见。这些误解不仅影响了中西方的交流与合作，也加深了全球人民之间的隔阂。

为了解决这些问题，我们需要更多的文化交流与对话。通过教育和媒体，我们可以传播更多关于中国的真实故事，展示中国人民的智慧、创造力和热情。只有在相互理解的基础上，世界各国才能真正实现和平与合作，共同面对全球性的挑战。

通过加强中西方之间的沟通与理解，我们不仅可以消除误解，增进友谊，还可以从彼此的经验中学习，创造一个更加包容和谐的世界。这不仅是对中国古老智慧的传承和弘扬，也是对现代中国的尊重与认可。

海庆中英文双语书店填补了这种文化和知识交流需求中的空白。在一个日益互联的世界中，不同文化之间的相互理解需求从未如此重要。这个书店作为桥梁，提供了从英语世界和中国古代智慧中获得的丰富知识和视角。

通过提供双语书籍，海庆使读者能够探索和欣赏中国文化和哲学的丰富性，同时也能接触当代全球的思想。这不仅有助于纠正对现代中国的误解和无知，还促进了不同背景人们之间的更深联系和共鸣。

本质上，海庆中英文双语书店解决了一个显著的空白，促进了一种更加包容和全面的学习和理解方法。对于任何想要拓宽视野，拥抱人类思想和经验多样性的人来说，它都是一个重要的资源。

敬请扫码进入海庆亚马逊中英文双语书店，沉浸于自由的双语言的新的觉醒。